"During a long career in naval intelligence, Admiral Studeman gained his reputation as one of the foremost analysts of China. Now, drawing on insights from years in command, he reveals himself to be a serious thinker on the nature of leadership as well. This is a thoughtful and engaging book."

Dr. Henry Kissinger
Secretary of State 1973–1977

"There are countless books available on leadership. *Might of the Chain* by Admiral Mike Studeman is distinctly different as well as succinct and eminently readable. The book is a distillation of leadership lessons learned over the course of a long and successful career in the Navy. In brief, incisive chapters, Studeman discusses the many characteristics of a good leader along with short stories highlighting the importance of each. The book is very personal, the stories ranging from poignant and moving to funny and informative. The reader learns a lot not only about leadership but the intelligence profession and national security. I've read a lot of books about leadership and have written one myself. *Might of the Chain* is quite special."

Robert M. Gates
Secretary of Defense 2006–2011

"This leadership book is superb, beautifully written, and quite engrossing."

Admiral Jim Stavridis, USN (Ret.)
Supreme Allied Commander, NATO 2009–2014,
author of *To Risk It All: Nine Crises and the Crucible of Decision*

"Before you can be a leader of others you must learn to lead yourself. Studeman's examples are gems with universal applications that can help take you wherever you want to go in life. Highly recommended."

Stephen Coonts
author of *Flight of the Intruder*
and 15 other *New York Times* bestselling novels

"Thoughtful and engaging"
–Dr. Henry Kissinger

MIGHT
OF THE
CHAIN

Forging Leaders of Iron Integrity

MIKE STUDEMAN
Rear Admiral, U.S. Navy (Ret.)

STONE TOWER PRESS

Might of the Chain: Forging Leaders of Iron Integrity
Copyright © 2024 Mike Studeman
All rights reserved.

The views expressed in this publication are those of the author and do not necessarily reflect the official policy or position of the Department of Defense or the U.S. government. The public release of this publication by the Department of Defense does not imply Department of Defense endorsement or factual accuracy of the material.

Stone Tower Press
7 Ellen Rd.
Middletown, RI 02842
stonetowerpress.com

ISBN: 979-8-9894008-3-6

Cover and text design by: Amy Cole, JPL Design Solutions

Printed in the United States of America

For my sons, Noah and Joshua,
who deserve a better world, and ways to make it so

CONTENTS

INTRODUCTION

Scarcely known beyond the worlds of the U.S. and British maritime communities are the "Laws of the Navy." The 27 Laws were authored in 1896 by Lieutenant Ronald A. Hopwood, later admiral, who was once called the "poet laureate of the Royal Navy." The Laws crossed over into U.S. Navy parlance in the 1920s and still today offer foundational naval wisdom to every midshipman, officer, and sailor about the values, principles, and expectations of their naval profession.

The most trenchant and memorable Fifth Law of the Navy goes:

> On the strength of one link of the cable,
> Dependeth the might of the chain.
> Who knows when thou may'st be tested?
> So live that thou may bearest the strain!

Experienced mariners know everything on a ship must work in harmony because hazards are ever present. Operating mammoth machines on the wild seas while keeping life support, propulsion, navigation, and combat systems in good working order requires synchronicity by all hands. A sailor's challenges are legion, from the latent tendency of complex systems to break down anywhere anytime on the planet, to dangers in hostile waters from foreign navies, air forces, missile networks, maritime militia, pirates, terrorists, and well-armed criminal groups, to the ocean herself, which always seems keen on sinking anything that dares trespass the briny deep. Skillfulness, teamwork, and a shared devotion to a higher calling keep ships functioning smoothly, steaming confidently ahead, and fulfilling their mission design.

Sailors know from hard experience that every link matters. They know every person must shoulder their load and live out the creed of mutual trust or the team founders. They view codependency as an analog to the integrity of an anchor chain. Fleet sailors aboard our capital ships in the U.S. Navy could tell you a Nimitz-class aircraft carrier anchor chain is comprised of almost 700 links weighing 350 pounds each, which can be paid out the length of almost five football fields. A failure of any single link along that enormous length and a 100,000-ton carrier might not only lose a 60,000-pound anchor but find itself at the mercy of the wind, waves, and current. Absent extraordinary effort to quickly power back up and regain headway, even the most powerful vessels can find themselves on the rocks.

While there are many strong links in our society, the sailor's lesson is that it only takes a few weak ones for breakage and runaway problems to emerge. Links snapping under strain can cause serious damage. People can get hurt, companies can go under, nations can struggle. The heavier the chain, the more load on the links, the more catastrophic the potential impact from flying shrapnel, and the harder it is to recover from ensuing drift.

It turns out every organization and every institution needs their mighty chain. And mighty chains must have mighty links, leaders of iron integrity connected up and down the line. Quality leadership at all levels, not just at the top, repeatedly proves to be the key differentiator between whether individuals, organizations, or endeavors struggle or become truly great. Leading with integrity across the sweep of an organization equips it to bear the strains of its environment, withstand supreme stress at any point, and operate at peak performance no matter ever-present pressures.

Disturbingly, our nation faces a crisis of leadership today. Polls are showing record low confidence in people occupying senior positions across all sectors of our society. A 2023 Gallup poll showed only 21% of American workers trust their leaders.[1] Further, 80% of respondents agreed there was a leadership crisis in both the U.S. government and corporate America.[2] Almost 60% of polled Americans agreed that

"I don't see any leaders at my company today that I aspire to be."[3] Barely 15% trust Washington to do what is right most of the time. A mere 2% expressed a great deal of trust and confidence in Congress.[4] Only 1 in 3 trust mass media. Even confidence in the U.S. military is at its lowest in 25 years.[5] Leaders across the board are not living up to their promise, not necessarily because their political philosophies are different, but because their attitudes, abilities, moral core, comportment, or actions have fallen short of expectations.

Trust in authority figures has been dwindling since the 1960s, but it has plummeted to nadir in recent years because Americans simply don't see their leaders consistently doing the right thing. Americans expect their leaders to acknowledge citizens' fears, uncertainties, challenges, and frustrations. Americans expect their leaders to work together to produce common-sense solutions to their problems. They expect forward progress. They expect timely results. They expect leaders to find opportunities for people to elevate their lives. They expect their leaders to demonstrate the maturity to rise above the omnipresent animus and discord to find ways to advance our society into the future.

When progress along all those lines is elusive, people naturally become more insecure. They sense dangers crowding around, whether real, imagined, or fabricated for calculated effect. They feel a world becoming more Hobbesian. Together, those feelings can reanimate a primitive instinct to seek safety and security in one's respective tribe. As people become more inward to seek protection, they often turn to strongmen they think might deliver better results. Tribe members in these circumstances will do almost anything to avoid being abandoned by their tribe, including adhering to putative mantras and self-talk (factual or otherwise) that circulate in those echo chambers. Unfortunately, in these conditions, it is also true that many promising leaders become reluctant to leave their tribes to compete for greater public service positions because they seem to offer only vicious chaos. Our country finds itself amid this ongoing societal disintegration and talent retrenchment.

America cannot afford to let these trends continue. Questionable leadership on the national scene has already induced too much drag on our democracy. The compounding crises of divisiveness, obsession with culture wars, civil unraveling abetted by disinformation, and failure to compromise for the common good have kept our ship of state only inching along at times, imperiled in shoal water.[6] Inadequate leaders in key positions have already radiated excessive damage and embrittlement along their arcs of influence, amplifying disenchantment and disengagement in the land. Short-sighted American leaders created these problems and only superb leaders can now fix the dysfunction.

Developing enlightened leaders in our country is not just an academic issue carrying local implications. We cannot hope to deal with the increasingly dangerous complexities of the modern era or advance our collective well-being with anything less than high-caliber people able to apply inspiring, knowledgeable, ethical, and inclusive leadership. Our shared struggles are colossal, whether confronting existential malignant ones like climate change and global health, or facing the reality of geopolitical backsliding into a world of conflicting power blocs pitting tyrannical autocracies against liberal democracies.

Sage leadership has always been the hidden secret of our success as a nation. But we are overdue for a revitalization of this skill across the American polity and within the fabric of our society. We can no longer assume that quality leadership just happens or that it magically appears when someone attains a certain rank, title, or position of influence. We all have to work at it and the labor never ends. The best leaders perpetually strive to make tomorrow's performance better than yesterday's.

For all these reasons and more, it is worth re-emphasizing the importance of leading well with good character, respect, civility, factual information, and moral courage. We need to get back to being well-versed in leadership basics. We need to hold ourselves accountable for being a strong, contributory link. And we need to hold one another accountable for doing so as well.

This compilation of lessons extracts the most important take-aways from a lifetime of study and practice of leading in the national security environment through turbulent times. I am far from a perfect leader, but I know what right looks like and I know what it takes to lead with integrity. By integrity I mean the most fulsome definition of the word: (1) the quality of being honest, (2) having strong moral principles, and (3) the state of being whole and undivided. Both individuals and organizations succeed when they exercise the true meaning of integrity and both invariably fail without it.

Organized inside out, this book is broken into three major segments highlighting the importance of first forging oneself (becoming a stainless-steel link), shaping one's team (joining alloyed chains), and ultimately transforming the world around us (lifting great weights). More simply, the three parts follow the general trajectory of most leadership journeys from the forge to the foundry to the field; from individual development to team building to deploying leadership capability for good effect.

Each chapter offers an illustration, a true story from my circle of experiences that exemplify a particular leadership characteristic or trait. Each story ends with extracts from leadership "minutes" I sent to thousands of military members and civilian intelligence professionals of all ranks in numerous organizations I was privileged to lead around the world. Those thoughts on leadership could be read in less than 60 seconds and served as jump-off points for thoughtful conversations in the ranks. What benefited these busy "doers" serving their nation can also serve you, serve us, as we try to live up to our obligation to convert axioms of leadership into more positive, purposeful action in our own orbits. To be the leader you should be. To become a leader who, above all, elevates everything in your midst.

Inspiring, effective, honorable leadership profits everything and everyone it touches. It's the high-grade steel in your chain. The opposite is also true. Poor leadership is the rust, corrosion, and cracking that threatens to shatter links and create unwanted drift on dangerous seas. Use this work to further strengthen your rigging, empower your people, and watch your organization and aspirations reach new heights as you achieve more bearing capacity, higher morale, and better outcomes, faster. The strains are upon us. Much is at stake.

How strong is your individual link?

How strong is your organization's chain?

FORGING YOUR SELF

BECOMING A LINK OF STAINLESS STEEL

A leader must be their own metalworker first, a blacksmith immersed in the furnace heat hammering away with sparks flying at their own molten glow. Chapters in this first section focus on developing the underlying qualities, attitudes, and skills of worthy leaders, the equivalent of firing, quenching, and tempering microstructures of one's metal until it becomes a strong, durable material fit to absorb the loads of its designed purpose. The best leaders forge themselves into a kind of stainless steel, something offering supreme strength, an ability to withstand extreme temperatures, and high resistance to life's corrosion and abrasion. Of course, stainless steel is also aesthetically attractive, a beauty that can sustain itself over time, always reflecting light into its world.

1
STARTING OUT

"Twenty years from now you will be more disappointed by the things you didn't do than by the ones you did. So throw off your bowlines. Sail away from safe harbor. Catch the trade winds in your sail. Explore. Dream. Discover."[7]

– Sarah Frances Brown

Beginning a career can be scary, but there's no hiding from the challenges of life. The sooner you confront them, the sooner you'll learn to deal with them. Each small victory and every challenge met will build confidence, skills, and knowledge, and set you on a path to unlock more of your true potential.

I started out in the Navy in 1988, inspired by the book *The Flight of the Intruder* by Stephen Coonts and stirred by a life of service to the nation that I observed in my father as he rose through the officer ranks. I attended Officer Candidate School during a frigid winter in Newport, Rhode Island, received my commission, and then attended an Intelligence Officer Basic Course in Virginia Beach.

In my first year in the Navy, I saw the world changing fast. Within five months, the Chinese Communist Party massacred students in Tiananmen Square to silence a democratic movement in the East and the Berlin Wall fell in a new burst of freedom in the West.

In my first assignment, I found myself in my dream job as an Air Intelligence Officer for an A-6 Intruder squadron out of Oceania,

Virginia. The A-6 was a two-seat, carrier-based, all-weather, day/night, low-level, long-range attack aircraft designed to deliver 18,000 pounds of ordnance through heavy enemy air defenses. A-6s were 1960s-vintage and had seen action in Vietnam.

I was obsessed with flying and the squadron leadership sportingly approved me to qualify to fly in the bombardier/navigator side seat in addition to my primary intelligence responsibilities. I ended up with a total of 40 hours of flying in the jet, much of it catapulting off and trapping on the deck of the USS *Saratoga* (CV-60). I couldn't believe my luck, mixing the work of intelligence with amazing aviation experiences. As an ensign, it was a thrilling introduction to the Navy.

Then Saddam Hussein invaded Kuwait, the most significant act of aggression in the new post-Cold War environment. Life got serious fast. Our aircraft carrier strike group immediately steamed across the Atlantic, through the Mediterranean and Suez Canal to our station in the sweltering Red Sea between Egypt and Saudi Arabia for Operations Desert Shield and Desert Storm.

During a pre-Christmas port visit in Haifa, Israel, a local liberty boat that was poorly piloted in heavy seas capsized late at night as it was returning 100 sailors to the aircraft carrier. 19 shipmates tragically drowned that night. I still remember standing on the deck of the carrier watching Israeli jets streak across the sky, helicopters circle between ship and shore, and flares light up the night as rescuers tried to find and pull sailors out of the dark, cold water.

Three weeks later, when Saddam refused to withdraw from Kuwait by a mid-January 1991 deadline, we faced off against combat-tested Iraqi forces, the fourth largest military in the world. I was charged with tracking Iraqi ground, air, and air defense forces, strike planning, and mission briefs and debriefs. My squadron mates flew off the carrier from the Red Sea, crossed the wide expanse of Saudi Arabia, and executed dangerous combat missions in Iraq and Kuwait against some of the world's most sophisticated air defenses.

Lieutenant Commander (Lt. Cdr) Scott Speicher from a sister F/A-18 squadron was shot down and killed by an Iraqi fighter on the first night of the war. On night two, Lt. Bob Wetzel and Lt. Jeff Zaun from our squadron were shot down by a surface-to-air missile (SAM) during a low-level attack in western Iraq and held as prisoners of war. We didn't know Bob had survived until after the war. The same day, Lt. John Snevely and Lt. Mark Eddy's A-6 was also hit by a SAM, forcing an emergency landing in Saudi Arabia. On the fourth day of the war, Lt. Devon Jones and Lt. Larry Slade's F-14 Tomcat was downed by another missile. Devon was dramatically rescued while Larry became a POW, interrogated, and tortured. When Devon arrived back on the ship a couple of days later, he had no white in his eyes, just orbs of black and red from where all his blood vessels burst from the incredible negative g-forces of the Tomcat in a flat spin before he could eject. All told, during Desert Storm, America lost 33 aircraft in combat; 148 Americans were killed in action.

The gravity of risky naval operations on any given day, and then war, exposed the life and death business in which I found myself. This was not what I expected to face as an ensign: the first major American war since Vietnam, losing friends and teammates, not knowing who would come back to the ship. I would watch brave naval aviators launch off the deck with a pit in my stomach every time, praying our intelligence support was accurate enough to give them the best chance of success. After multiple crews were shot down, I carried unshakeable guilt that perhaps I hadn't done enough, hadn't figured out enemy movements in time to allow aircrews to avoid the worst dangers. Shouldn't I have helped figure out that traditional low-level attacks by A-6E Intruders through thick anti-aircraft artillery (AAA) and short-range missile systems might not be as safe as higher altitude operations against this particular mix of Iraqi, Soviet, and French air defense equipment?

Like many young men and women at the time, who were greenhorns in life, I was both untested and unready for what I faced. But in the middle of combat operations, we knew for the sake of others that we needed to rise to the occasion. Circumstances simply demanded it. Most of us matured many years in just those 100 days and were forever changed.

Trials by fire can come early. What I learned is that people can do more than they think themselves capable. We don't know our true faculties until we face powerful forces we would never otherwise voluntarily invite into our lives. I drew on those experiences in 1991 for the rest of my career. Armed with an intimate understanding of the consequences of getting intelligence right for men and women in uniform, I drove myself to be the best intelligence officer I could be for another three and a half decades of service. Desert Storm unveiled my greatest self-doubts, but ultimately it also became my deepest source of strength, because it opened my eyes to the value and impact of being supremely excellent in all that we do.

> Forging ahead requires a willingness to be shaped by forces out of our control, just as an unyielding block of metal is eventually transformed blow by blow into something functional by fire, hammer, and anvil.

> Becoming truly effective hinges on an unrelenting eagerness to learn the arcane secrets of your guild, taking any assignment that can convey the tradecraft secrets of experienced craftsmen in your chosen profession.

> Brace for trials by fire. Steel yourself for intense struggles, surprises, and failures, and know that's where the best education awaits.

> Get used to ever-present stresses and know that pressure is a cooperative precondition for high performance.

2

ACCOUNTABILITY

"The possession of great power necessarily implies great responsibility."

– William Lamb

I learned an unforgettable early lesson in accountability as an 11-year-old when I lived in Italy with my family. My father was a commander in the U.S. Navy assigned to the Sixth Fleet staff, which was headquartered on an aging cruiser, the USS *Albany* (CG 10). The ship was home-based in Gaeta, Italy, two hour's drive north of Naples.

We lived on the third and fourth floors of an apartment, which sat at the convergence of two streets in the center of town. American families occupied four corners of the apartment building; the local landlord and family, the first two floors.

As you might imagine, expatriate families in a foreign country create strong bonds. I was particularly close to the three Campisi brothers. I was the oldest of the three, David was a year younger than me, Mark two years younger, and Kevin the youngest at seven.

One lazy afternoon, I invented a game for us where we each took turns rolling marbles off the fourth-story balcony, aiming them toward the street trash cans to see who could hit them and make the loudest sound during siesta hours. We took delight if the crashing noise also sent stray cats streaking away. My only rule was to not throw a marble at a parked car or if a car was driving by.

Most of our marbles harmlessly bounced on the road or were lost out of sight in the trees and back plots of the neighbors' yards. The game was harder than it looked.

About ten minutes into this challenge, we heard the sound of a speeding car approaching, the driver clearly in a hurry. It was a shiny black Mercedes gunning through town. Younger Kevin was in a position to launch his marble and was concentrating on making a good roll. I'll never forget the serious look on his face, his tongue pushing a bulge below his mouth as he stared across the street. Just as I was about to warn him of the approaching car, his arm unleashed a doozy, the marble whizzing under the rails, the glass ball sparkling in the sun as it arced outward in the air.

Everything went into slow motion. I yelled a long "Nooooo!" as the marble plummeted toward the street. I heard the car engine roaring closer and watched the vehicle speed behind the line of trees shading the edge of our apartment complex. Suddenly a loud shattering sound, a screeching of tires—errrr, errrr, errrr—and a huge crashing noise as the car plowed through the metal trash cans, our former targets.

I muttered an expletive and yelled "Inside, inside, inside!" grabbing as many Campisi boy arms as I could. We tumbled into the dark room and quickly slammed shut the sliding wooden doors. Our hearts beat wildly and we were all breathing hard, nobody saying a word. Everyone stared at me.

The local Italian police wasted no time tracking down the culprits. They knocked on the Campisi door first, got the full story from the brothers, and then knocked on our apartment door. We learned that the car belonged to the mayor of Gaeta! We were not arrested due to our age, but I was ultimately responsible for paying for a new windshield. My parents told me that was all on me. It took me more than a summer's worth of babysitting for other American families around town to pay back what I owed. It was one of my first serious lessons in being accountable for one's actions.

> A responsible leader absorbs any buffeting no matter how violent the turbulence and no matter the personal or professional costs.[8]

> Real leaders live by a time-tested covenant with their people that acknowledges that obligations come hand-in-hand with power—investiture confers both title and duty.

> Those in positions of power who demonstrate an unwillingness to take accountability for their actions, or the choices of those they lead, bring a pox on their leadership house.

> A leader who truly stands tall is one ready to take a fall, to own either victory or loss with equanimity.

3

CHARISMA

*"Charisma is not about being the center of attention:
it's about making others feel seen and valued."*

– Oprah Winfrey

Where you find them, leaders with an admirable blend of charisma, competence, and character are a marvel to watch. They win support, they get things done, and they take the right action. My father-in-law, the Reverend James Draper, was one of those people, someone who deployed his innate charisma for noble ends. Since the 1960s, he served as a leader of communities, an itinerant United Methodist Minister who never spent more than five years in any one church in Virginia. He led a dozen parishes over his forty-year career, serving thousands of lay people in towns and villages across the state. He was a great American and an even greater community leader.

Pastor Jim was blessed with the gift of the gab, all dressed in his southern Virginia drawl. He would charm at every turn. Interacting with people fed him like it does many extroverts, but he delivered more abundantly back to those around him. In his ministrations, he was an inexhaustible provider of faith-based inspiration, life counsel, and comfort. He provided the treasure of his time and attention in countless hospitals, providing prayer and companionship to those suffering or near the end of life. He would hearten the disheartened.

He knew all about human sins, foibles, and frailties, but demonstrated unconditional compassion for both transgressors and the wronged.

You knew when Jim entered a room. His big personality radiated sunshine and warmth. He'd poke fun, draw smiles, and skip into the small joys in people's lives, remembering little facts about people's families and their goings on. He used his gift of charisma and humor to make others feel seen, accepted, and special, no matter their circumstances.

Pastor Jim died from COVID-19 in Suffolk, Virginia in 2020, leaving a large emptiness in the hearts of his family, friends, and former parishioners. One day, I discovered a box in our house that contained all his sermon notes over the years. I could almost hear his voice as I sifted through homily after homily, reminding me of his gift for both connecting with people and opening their minds to a preacher's teachings. The culmination of one sermon captured the essence of the man and how he lived: "The only way we can follow in true discipleship is through the complete and utter giving of self in devotion to help another. The demonstration of this self-giving love releases the strongest influence, reaps the greatest harvests, and redeems the hardest heart."

As a community leader, Pastor Jim understood the responsibility that comes hand-in-hand with authority. He knew a vibrant personality can be a powerful asset for leaders when properly paired with character, competence, and a worthy cause. He also knew the ills of unmoored charisma, the kind he witnessed inspire fear, hate, division, and incivility in his country in the last years of his life. Like any reservoir of talent, charisma can help cure or contaminate, depending on the nature of the vessel it is carried in.[9]

> Charisma involves employing the most colorful fetches of one's personality, untethering the power of one's unique interpersonal allure to captivate interest and followership.

> Anyone can further develop their confidence, conviction, and vitalities to create more soft power and influence with others.

> Charisma can be deployed for either virtuous or dishonorable ends. Charisma without the undercarriages of good character, noble cause, and factual information will lead followers down warped and dangerous paths.

> Responsible charismatic leaders understand that they are not selling themselves, but the value they provide to others.

4

CHARACTER

"If you have integrity, nothing else matters.
If you don't have integrity, nothing else matters."

– Senator Alan Simpson

I've worked for many impressive leaders with strong moral fiber over the years, but Charlie Allen is the best exemplar of character I've ever witnessed. A veteran of the CIA, Charlie devoted 65 years of his life to the nation as a government official. He joined the agency in 1958, worked for 13 CIA Directors, served as the President's Daily Briefer to multiple Presidents, National Intelligence Officer for Counter-Terrorism and Warning, and was Assistant Director of Central Intelligence for Collections.

Charlie was one of those people with a knack for walking with history. His legendary career spanned the Cuban Missile Crisis to the post-9/11 Global War on Terror. He was an intrepid Cold War warrior who rose through the ranks as an analyst, collection manager, and covert action planner. He interacted with the President and National Security Staff principals during the Yom Kippur War in 1973 and the Iran-Contra affair in the mid-1980s. He predicted and warned about Saddam Hussein's intent to invade Kuwait in 1990. He was a counterterrorist expert who understood the dangers of Al Qaeda, especially after the twin bombings of U.S. embassies in Kenya and Tanzania in 1998, and was the first to advocate arming Predators to go after Osama Bin Laden before 9/11. Charlie was an integral member of the inner circle of advisors devising options in the immediate aftermath of 9/11 and then supported the deployment of CIA agents into Afghanistan to connect with the Northern Alliance and overthrow the Taliban regime that harbored Al Qaeda.

Charlie had a reputation as irascible, iron-willed, and charismatic. One colleague once described him as a "brilliant man" with a "yen for controversy."[10] He was also renowned for his unimpeachable moral courage and willingness to speak truth to power, whether advising CIA Directors, other agency leaders, or those in the Oval Office.[11] He didn't suffer fools lightly and he always spoke his mind. He was a patriot's patriot, one whose loyalty to the constitution and country transcended his loyalty to any one official, no matter their rank or title.

After serving for over a half-century for the CIA, he became the Chief of Intelligence and Undersecretary for Intelligence and Analysis at the young Department of Homeland Security (DHS). I was assigned to DHS soon after being selected as a White House Fellow in 2005 and it was there at the Nebraska Ave headquarters in northwest Washington that Charlie brought me on as his Special Assistant. I was crossing the campus one afternoon after participating in a President's Hurricane Katrina Recovery Task Force meeting when he stopped me and declared "Mike, you now work for me!"

I didn't have a choice in the matter, nor did I want one. I had briefly interacted with Charlie when soliciting his support to help track Chinese submarines. I instantly liked the cut of his jib. He lived up to his reputation as a tough, energetic, 80-hour-a-week "doer" who relished orchestrating creative solutions to seemingly impossible problems. He moved the needles on hard challenges, cow-prodding reluctant bureaucracies to focus on the right things.

At age 67, Charlie faced new mountains to climb at DHS. I had a front-row seat as he employed every technique to create a true intelligence enterprise out of disparate intelligence arms of DHS.[12] Less than two years young, the department's whole was not yet greater than the sum of its parts. It was not ready to fulfill its mandate to rapidly share and fuse information between private, tribal, territorial, local, state, and federal entities to respond to all hazards and all dangers to the homeland. Charlie assumed the daunting task of coordinating and synchronizing the information sharing efforts in and beyond the new Department, which was comprised of nine organizations with their own intelligence services at the federal level alone.[13]

Charlie eventually built a church organ out of this scattered stack of stovepipes. For me, it was a master class in executive leadership in action. While I learned about business practices, organizational techniques, and process improvement; while I learned about the importance of intermixing the attractive force of charm and the directive force of authority; and while I learned about the power of deploying the English language for effect (Charlie was the king of colloquialisms), what struck me was how Charlie inspired change by virtue of his character. He had gravitas because he was honorable and well-intentioned, which engendered trust. He had throw-weight because he insisted on doing the right thing for the right reasons, which earned respect. He was effective because he delivered tough love while maintaining the dignity of those he tutored, which inspired active followership.

I always knew instinctively that one's character is the foundation of leadership, but what Charlie demonstrated was how those moral components converted to indispensable sources of influence when handling epically tough issues. He pulled people into his slipstream mainly because the underlying excellence of his character inspired trust and confidence. People ended up doing extraordinary things to realize Charlie's vision at DHS, and they did so because he was admirable to the core.

> If your decisions rest on a bedrock of integrity, you will succeed in life because people will gravitate toward those who are well-anchored, who have an ethical vitality, and who are fundamentally decent.[14]

> Building trust with others grows out of confidence not just in your professional competence, but your ability to convince others you are well-intentioned, fair, and genuinely concerned about your colleagues' welfare.

> Acting from an ethical foundation means always demonstrating honesty, sincerity, integrity, and personal accountability.

> Your true character shows up in every habit, a measure of moral excellence that registers the moment you make a choice.

5

AUTHENTICITY

*"Real development is not leaving things behind, as on
a road, but drawing life from them, as on a root."*

– G. K. Chesterton

I never thought I'd find an example of authenticity running shirt-less on a beach in Miami. Robert "Raven" Kraft, who got his nick-name from wearing all black in High School, has run eight miles a day on the sands of South Beach since 1975. His running streak has added up to over 140,000 miles, running through "hurricanes, pneu-monia, animal attacks, a nail-impaled foot, sciatica, concussions, bone spurs, vertigo, and food poisoning."[15] Over 3,600 people from every state and over 80 countries have run with him over the years. Raven's self-discipline and endurance are legendary in Miami. A living icon, he's been the subject of a documentary, book, and numer-ous sports articles. It is not too inaccurate to describe his following as cult-like.

Shortly after moving to Miami in 2017 for my first job as an admiral, my wife handed me a book called *Running with Raven* that she spied in a Coral Gables bookstore. "Have you heard of this guy?" I hadn't, but as an avid runner, I was instantly intrigued. In the early 1970s, when he was 19, Raven aspired to become a singer and song-writer and visited Nashville to learn from accomplished artists. A now-famous musician stole one of his draft songs from that trip, leaving Raven embittered. Back in Miami, Raven ultimately joined boxers from Fifth Street gym, where Muhammed Ali had trained, on beach runs. Those runs gave Raven a salve for his anger, a routine, and a newfound level of fitness. He made a New Year's resolution to run 365 consecutive days. That goal eventually expanded to running 10 years straight, then to reaching 100,000 miles. As of this writing, he's still fast-walk jogging eight miles a day, even though it sometimes takes him three hours, finishing well past sunset.[16]

Two weeks later after our bookstore discovery, I rendezvoused with Raven at his fixed start point at the Fifth Street lifeguard station at 5:15 p.m. He ambled up in his signature outfit of black running shorts, black headband, black socks, and a single black glove on one hand. Raven was medium-height, barrel-chested, wiry, and tanned. He was the fittest 67-year-old I'd seen. His black hair was tousled down to a curly mullet, his beard two-toned white and black, dark vertical stripes under his lip and extending down from the ends of his mustache dividing the lighter parts. I could see why he was caricatured as the "Forrest Gump of Miami." I felt like I had stepped onto a movie set and a director was about to film a hero scene.

In the last twenty years, as he became more famous, Raven has very rarely run alone. People from all walks of life and from all over the world have joined him to partake in his living legend-making. A record 280 other runners joined him when he passed his 100,000-mile mark in 2009. I was one of seven to join him this evening in the softening, pinking light. Raven did a roll call early in the run as we shuffled along the hard-packed sand, acknowledging those who already earned a call sign. Raven is reputed to have a near-photographic memory, recalling the call sign of everyone who has ever run with him. Tonight, "Hurricane," an 87-year former mail fraud felon, was checked in. Raven jokingly described him as "Category Zero." Next a former baseball star ("Hitter"), a black bare-footed physical therapist ("Sheik"), a quiet 20-something ("Applicator"), and a 50-something man who lived on a 42-foot Morgan somewhere in Key Biscayne ("Sailboat"). Two of us were first-timers and didn't earn a call sign until after the run. A Texan mother of five on vacation, who Raven learned during the run had finished two Ironman triathlons in Mexico, eventually received the call sign "Miss Fit." She was all smiles. Raven inquired about my life as a military brat and issued me "Wanderlust" at the end. I was runner 2,966.

During the run, Raven was unrushed, listening attentively, occasionally asking questions, offering a story here and there. All the locals waved at him, the lifeguards on four-wheelers zipping home at the end of their workday, the workers folding up beach umbrellas, well-to-do locals on their evening constitutional, even the beach bums settling into their favored notches in the shadowed dunes. He was the grittiest celebrity of Miami.

That was the first of several runs I did with Raven, each as surreal as the last. Something vaguely spiritual was at work. It wasn't just the sand and ocean. It wasn't the eerie glow of sunsets slowly becoming enveloped by the neon lights blinking on from art deco hotels and restaurants, or revelers emerging to join South Beach's famed nightlife. Raven was living his authentic life and offering others to live theirs. The call signs he gave were a reflection of their lives well-lived. Anyone could accompany him on his daily sabbatical and be accepted on their own terms. Pretenses could drop, and masks could melt away. Raven was the genuine article, living life as he chose to architect it, inspiring others to do the same. Raven was a one-man community builder who offered congruity to an incongruous crowd, concord among the usually discordant. His was an unlikely club of eclectics, a motley crew. Membership came from just showing up. He connected strikingly divergent individuals, who had nothing in common except a shared desire to participate in something valiant, pure, natural.[17]

Laura Lee Huttenbach, call sign "White Lightning," authored *Running with Raven* and logged over 1,000 miles with him. She observed, "When I started running with Raven, I noticed one thing that people seem to have in common that were with him was that they were either striving to be more authentic to themselves or they just were more authentic individuals. And that was really attractive to me to see just a group of people that was trying to be closer to themselves and who they were."[18]

Raven eventually lived out his dream to become a singer-song-writer. He's released three albums with titles like *The Road is Long* and *Unstoppable*. He sings bass, like his hero Johnny Cash. One of his song lyrics goes "Let me be your restoration and do eight miles with me."

Over the decades, Raven has become one of the most constant fixtures in Miami's splashy and ever-dynamic scenery, never losing his sense of true self or ascetic nature even amid the endless indulgencies of the Magic City. He continues to spend his popularity on others, helping every runner who ventures down to the Fifth Street lifeguard station to see that they, too, can become their own legend. Raven demonstrates each day in his unappointed leadership role that the journey to greatness lies in living in the closest accord with one's genuine identity, one's most mature authentic self.

> How you carry yourself and what comes from your lips must ring true, it must conform to your personality, temperament, and life experiences. It has to fit into your format.

> Subordinates don't want artificial leaders or actors playing a part. They want authentic bosses, people comfortable in their skins.

> Bringing out the best in our leadership talent does not mean casting lines off from our past. It should be a honing, not a disowning process.

> Absorb lessons and expand your skills, but put your imprint on any borrowed device.

6

VIGOR

"The health and vigor necessary for the practice of what is good, depends equally on both mind and body."

– Diogenes

I accidentally discovered the true power of physical conditioning as it relates to professional capability. Although I swam and played soccer as a kid, I was only a junior varsity runner on my high school track and cross-country team. I fenced in college and was a two-time Mid-Atlantic Fencing Association epee champion at the end of my junior and senior years at the College of William & Mary, but I was only ever a second alternate to the NCAA. You could say I was a middle-of-the-road athlete in my youth, always trying hard, but never gifted with a sports gene that was worthy of brag-worthy heroism. I was OK with that. I enjoyed being on teams, partaking in competitions, and trying my best.

Perhaps because I enjoyed so few athletic claims to fame earlier in life, I continued to push myself as a runner, joining 5K and occasional 10K races. I never took home any medals. Ever curious about other sports, I eventually tried sprint triathlons, which usually involved borrowing a ten-speed bike from my girlfriend (eventually wife). No podiums there either. My usual routine was a solo run 3–4 times a week exploring different routes wherever I lived, content to trudge around for over an hour. I knocked out a marathon in my thirties.

I wasn't ever fast or great, but I was certainly consistent in staying in shape and getting my workouts in. I kept prioritizing this part of my life for decades, no matter how intense my jobs became. I protected that side of my life because I believed strongly in the Greek sense of the mutually supporting interrelatedness of mind, body, and spirit. I wanted to be healthy, hale, and whole as a person. I also knew that staying physically fit acted as a source of attitudinal strength in other areas of my life.

In college, I had marveled at a show called the *Eco-Challenge*, advertised as the world's toughest race. It was a multi-day expedition adventure race composed of teams of four navigating hundreds of miles by compass and map alone in difficult, picturesque terrain all over the world. I vowed someday to do something like that. I picked up mountain biking in my forties and eventually realized I might be able to give the combined sport of adventure racing a try.

In my years as a commander in the Navy, I worked my way up through 5, 8, 12, 24, and 30-hour adventure races, which meant becoming proficient in orienteering, paddling, running, rappelling, and mountain biking. I would train late at night or on weekends around family events. At each event, I would regularly make serious mistakes regarding nutrition, land navigation, pace setting, and equipment. I learned the hard way with each event. The long hours at night, alone in wild terrain, miles away from the nearest human being, and often in bear and snake country tested my wits, courage, and physical tolerances in ways nothing else ever had. I liked the sport because it wasn't always the fastest athlete, but sometimes the cleverest one with smarter navigation choices, who placed well. I was jubilant when I finally won a solo category in the North American Adventure Racing Championship held in Pennsylvania in 2015, only to be humbled soon after when told that there was only one other solo entrant!

The epiphany I stumbled upon trying to discover my outer boundaries was that there are no fixed boundaries. Doing hard things allowed me to do more hard things. Every obstacle or challenge that was overcome built up my confidence, shifted my perspective on what was truly strenuous in life and generated a deep well of serenity. And being fit simply made me a calmer person at home, at work, and elsewhere.

I was competing in these endurance races as a middle-aged man while simultaneously taking on some of the toughest assignments of my career: serving as the senior intelligence officer afloat for a carrier strike group composed of multiple capital ships, an air wing of 70 aircraft, and 7,500 personnel engaging in contingency and combat support in the Middle East; commander of an intelligence unit composed of 900 civilian and military personnel; and special assistant to the Chief of Naval Operations (CNO).

In retrospect, I think I was able to handle those intense jobs with less stress and more determination because I could draw on a greater store of physical reserves and psychological composure. Whatever daring I mustered in races translated in professional work settings into feelings of self-possession, surety, and even a tad of fearlessness. I felt like I was more enterprising, creative, and energetic. I took more calculated risks and became more confident in my abilities even in the face of uncertainty and under what some might consider extreme pressure.

I found myself shrugging at long flights overseas on military executive jets working out and back between CNO engagements with the fleet and foreign partners overseas because I could compare them to 30 hours of no sleep while carrying a pack through miles of unforgiving wilderness. No boardroom meeting could ever get scarier than hearing a black bear growling 20 yards away while traversing thick rhododendron bushes alone in a valley. No project deadline on staff would make me sweat more than trying to figure out how to get back into an 8-person raft after being ejected into a boulder-strewn Class IV rapid.

For me, it took engaging in an extreme sport to truly understand the correlation between physical fitness and leadership capability. It's enough to say that any amount of physical stress and conditioning will likely help serve as a source of strength for anyone who partakes in it, because it raises one's pain tolerance and salves the spirit. My lesson was that striving to apply rigor in how one keeps in shape—a day-by-day priority choice—can directly add to one's self-assurance and level of indefatigability when engaged in work pursuits. Ultimately, it can be the difference between whether one is a net energy consumer in life or a net energy giver. I've found the most capable leaders fall into the latter category.

> - Elevating one's physical gameplay directly parlays into lifting one's professional gameplay. People recognize and are more willing to follow people who are vibrant and energetic.

> - Going to the edges of any form of suffering increases one's capacity to absorb it, rise above it, and then help others do the same.

> - One's grit correlates to the interplay of both psychological toughness and physical fortitude.

> - One's total fitness level magnifies one's capacity to withstand stress, demonstrate grace under pressure, and not just endure but bring life, hope, and fire to whatever needs to get done.

7
COMMUNICATION

"Courage is what it takes to stand up and speak;
courage is also what it takes to sit down and listen."

– Sir Winston Churchil

I learned hard lessons about the importance of good communication well before I joined the Navy. As a 12-year-old, I failed miserably at it with embarrassing consequences. It was another one of my many mishaps in Gaeta, Italy, where we lived in the late 1970s.

I grew up in a sailing family and have always been comfortable on the water. My father captained our family on a 24-foot sloop from Virginia down and back through the inter-coastal waterway to Key West one summer. We occasionally raced in rag-tag regattas on weekends in Hampton Roads.

Overseas in Gaeta, Navy families had access to the local marina located in the harbor opposite the U.S. Navy flagship, which was moored on a long concrete quay jutting into the small bay. My friends and I loved to run down to the docks after school in the summer and take out dinghies and knockabouts, which we could single or double-hand. I reveled in heeling the boats high on a close haul and repeatedly capsizing them so I would fall into the drink, a test of not getting wrapped in the main sheet or trapped under the sail, while earning the reward of a refreshing swim.

One weekend, Italian race organizers decided to pair older and younger kids together for a multi-class sailing regatta. I was volunteered an eight-year-old American boy named Daniel, who I didn't know very well, to crew with me on an Alpa Tris, a 12-foot open cockpit dinghy with a single crab claw, or oceanic lateen, sail rig. I wasn't too happy about the arrangement but kept my peace. I was a bit jealous of my older sister, Kim, who was invited to crew on a larger, faster Lightning class sailboat. But all we needed to do was complete a single lap around a three-buoy racecourse, which extended out beyond the bay at its farthest point.

After we launched from the pier, I didn't talk to Daniel much and simply directed him to various positions around the boat to make minor weight adjustments. He was thrilled by everything, but not familiar with boating, so I just used him like a moveable sack. I didn't review safety or emergency procedures, I didn't share my racing plan, and I didn't set expectations for how the boat would behave outside the protection of the harbor. I didn't even ask him much about himself or his family. Daniel was chattering away, doing talking for the both of us, pointing out all the sailboats dashing by in the hectic pre-race maneuvering by the start line.

The race committee boat blew the horn and we were quickly left behind by all of the other boats sprinting off. The Alpa Tris was the smallest and slowest sailboat in the race by a wide margin. The first leg was straight out of the bay to the far buoy, which turned out to be a relaxing downwind exit with the wind behind and waves heading out to sea. At the back of the pack, we watched small white swatches of sails tack around the first buoy in the distance.

The wind freshened and swells grew once we sailed beyond the shelter of the peninsula. Alone on the water with other sailboats now specks in the distance, exposed to more of the elements, with land receding away, Daniel began to get noticeably nervous. I found his reaction irritating, but I tried to reassure him we were fine. Turns out we weren't.

We finally passed the outer buoy and I attempted to go about to make for the next marker but failed again and again. The long roller swells heading out to sea were frustrating my ability to successfully tack. Our sea cow never gained enough speed for me to overcome both wind and waves. Even with the tiller hard over, each swell knocked the boat back, nosing us farther out to sea. I tried every trick in the book in terms of timing waves, sculling the tiller, throwing the boom over, and adjusting our weight on a favored side as we turned, all to no avail. After 15 minutes of trying increasingly desperate measures, now much further out to sea and in rougher seas, Daniel was an emotional puddle. I was so busy with the boat that I hadn't had time to manage his elevated anxiety.

We noticed a large white luxury yacht cruising by about a half mile away, the only other vessel out this far now. The powerboat was the most expensive in Gaeta: an 80-foot, multi-decked, teak-trimmed wonder owned by an Italian millionaire. It was the kind of vessel that could be featured on the cover of Boating Magazine. The powerboat was passing by and opening distance.

Suddenly, Daniel tore off his orange life jacket, stood up in our small dinghy, and frantically waved it over his head shouting "Aiuto! Aiuto! Aiuto!" ("help" in Italian). He was manic and wouldn't listen to my entreaties to sit back down and put his life jacket back on. This was now a major safety problem given the risk of tipping the boat and falling overboard. There would be no way for me to go back and pick him up if he lost his balance or got knocked over by the boom. I didn't know how well he could swim, especially in the churny offshore water.

Someone in the yacht party must have seen Daniel because the powerboat slowly turned toward us. Daniel was ecstatic with relief. Ugh, I thought, embarrassed that we looked like we needed rescuing. I just needed a little more time to pull off a tack.

The yacht should have approached from behind or parallel to my course, but it looked increasingly like the powerboat intended to cross the "t" in front of me, perpendicular to our direction of travel.

Holy smokes! The captain of the yacht seemed to assume I had more maneuverability than I did. Things happened fast. The powerboat motored forward and slowed to a stop directly downwind and down-wave from us. We would be on them in two swells. I yelled at Daniel to sit in the front of the boat and put his legs out to buffer any impact. I didn't have time to take down the sail. I tried to angle away from the yacht, but the powerboat was simply too wide and the last wave sent us hurtling right toward it. At the last second, naturally scared by the closing speed, Daniel pulled back his feet and hugged the mast. The bow of the dinghy hit the yacht's freeboard with a deep "thunk!" and I was thrown forward off the tiller.

Dazed, I looked up 15 feet to see an Italian crewman on deck. His eyes were wide with shock as he saw how much of our bow had stove in the powerboat's hull. It had penetrated so deeply that he had to grab the top of our mast and shake it back and forth to extract the dinghy's nose. We were taken aboard and the Alpa Tris was placed in tow for the tortuous ride back to the marina. I was mortified by the whole affair and it seemed even worse that the Italians turned out to be so kind and accommodating.

The skipper must have radioed ahead because Daniel's parents and many others were waiting at the slip. Daniel was on deck waving with excitement, while I hid behind a bulkhead, embarrassed by my profound failure. Of course, we moored to port with the gaping hole evident to the small crowd waiting for us.

I learned many lessons from that experience, many of them related to simple communication. I didn't establish any rapport with my younger shipmate. I didn't know him, his fears and confidences, or his skill level. Because I failed to build even a modicum of trust, it didn't exist, hence he ignored me when it mattered most. I had failed to review basic safety precautions. I had not set his expectations for what we were likely to face outside a calm harbor and didn't allow him to voice concerns or ask questions in advance. Moreover, I hadn't effectively reassured him as conditions became sportier, because I was consumed with independently solving the problem.

Long ago, I concluded that what we think is good enough communication is usually never good enough. It takes extraordinary effort to connect with people to the point of implicit trust, and both extroverts and introverts must constantly work to improve their listening and transmitting skills, respectively, no matter what mood they find themselves in. When you believe you are done, you have likely just started. The first and last order of business is to remain persistently engaged, smartly knowing when to use your ears or mouth.

> Good leaders don't master communication skills so much as they remain hyperconscious of exercising the most effective form of interactivity suitable to the conditions they face.

> People must be reassured leaders understand and care before the commerce of sincere communication can commence.

> Send clear signals and tailor your message to the audience. Brevity is king. Be pithy. Use words with economy. Provide ground truth in simple terms. Enliven imaginations and captivate interest through electric language, vivid imagery, and relatable storytelling.

> Dialoguing always takes a group farther than monologuing.

8

GROWTH

"It is what we make out of what we have, not what we are given, that separates one person from another."

– Nelson Mandela

The highest learning year of my life was when I was a White House Fellow. Our 2005–2006 Class was composed of 12 incredibly talented individuals from all walks of life. They were 20- and 30-somethings whose professions ranged from entrepreneur to doctor to lawyer to military officer, all who had shown promise as future leaders of significance through early career accomplishments and service to their respective communities. The combination of access to the highest levels of government, placement near cabinet-level leaders, engagements with notable Americans, and domestic/ international travel over a year offered a wealth of insights that I still find highly meaningful and relevant today. It was a rich time of learning, made more fruitful by the growing we did together as deeply bonded Fellows.

I learned the hard way not to be shy about reaching for opportunities like this. I had always been interested in a Federal Executive Fellowship, which military officers can apply for around their mid-career level for year-long assignments to think tanks or Federally Funded Research and Development Centers. I had read about the White House Fellows program in Colin Powell's autobiography *My*

American Journey but didn't think I could ever qualify for what was advertised as the country's most prestigious leadership program. That program was for special people—water walkers who thrived on some other plane of existence.

Then, one day, Commander Vince McBeth, a Surface Warfare Officer and former White House Fellow, caught up with me after a Navy conference where we had been wargaming certain scenarios with senior leaders. I had been the red team leader and presented highly challenging situations by a potential adversary to the senior Navy leaders in attendance. I faced significant flak in the hot wash-up review of the game, but patiently explained our opponent's doctrine, decision-making calculus, and military employment options.

I didn't know Vince, but he caught me walking out the door and recommended I apply to the White House Fellows program, offering to assist along the way. I thought he was bonkers. Vince had been the aide to the Secretary of the Navy, driven destroyers into the fraught waters of the Persian Gulf to enforce U.N. sanctions on Iraq, and was a former U.S. Naval Academy football star and captain of the team. I couldn't boast those kinds of extraordinary credentials.

I will always be grateful, however, that Vince pushed me with repeated promptings to apply. Although skeptical, I started the application process. Almost right off the bat, I was forced to put it on ice when I learned the Director of Naval Intelligence ordered me to be his intelligence representative to the Quadrennial Defense Review (QDR) Team. In 1997, Congress mandated an every four-year review of Defense Department strategy, priorities, and associated programs. The QDR was the predecessor of what became DoD's National Defense Strategy development process in 2018. The Navy would suffer or fare well from a resource standpoint, depending on how well our Service QDR team performed in the process. I was going to be locked in for at least a year with these new orders.

Vince wouldn't have any of it. He insisted I speak candidly with Rear Admiral Rick Porterfield, the Director of Naval Intelligence

(DNI), and solicit his support to continue the application process even while executing my QDR responsibilities. Pushed so, I reluctantly screwed up the courage to bring up this touchy subject with the head of my community. The DNI listened patiently to me in his Pentagon office, then to my surprise said, "Well, Mike, I know several people who've applied, but not made it. If you want to give it a try, go ahead. I'll let you go from QDR if you get lucky." I knew he knew the odds of me making it were slim, so he was inclined to offer moral support. Thank you, RADM Porterfield. Thank you, Vince.

Typically, up to 1,000 people from all over America apply to the White House Fellow program every year. Over months and to my surprise, I made it through the first application cut to 120 candidates, then the regional interviews cut to 30, then the national-level cut to the final 12 selected. The White House had already submitted our names to Congress for our official appointments when I got the congratulations call about three-quarters of the way through my QDR stint. Wow, I was thrilled!

The Navy QDR deputy director, a one-star admiral and flinty ship driver, heard the commotion in the office as my colleagues cheered. He strode in, half smiling, and said "I don't know, Mike. The Secretary of Defense has you committed through the end of QDR." Half smiling back, I said, "I don't know, he may need to talk to the President about that." Luckily, everyone, including the admiral, laughed. My teammates hooted and hollered.

My lesson is that we must sometimes break out of our shells to achieve growth. Vince compelled me to self-advocate against the normal forces that would have kept me tied into the Navy's harness. Chances to learn always seem to come at an inconvenient time and at some cost to the rhythm of our lives. So be it. We are the only ones truly in charge of our education. Those willing to pursue fleeting opportunities to "sharpen their saw," as Stephen Covey puts it, will invariably invest in greater-than-average success over the long haul. It's worth figuring out how to tap into the wisdom of the world. It's usually not found solely in the traditional circles we run, but somewhere beyond our comfortable lifelines. We just have to want it enough to lift out of the routine and transport ourselves there.

> The most promising professionals in any line of work are those who commit themselves to constant and never-ending improvement, possess an unquenchable curiosity about life, pursue a wide set of interests, and show a willingness to try new things.[19]

> As a fisher for your own development, you will always be well-served by casting your knowledge nets widely and hauling up a diverse catch of insights.

> Exposure to a diverse spectrum of readings, people, and experiences stimulates neurons, strengthens imaginative powers, and draws insight from the seemingly oblique.

> Finding exponential learning opportunities calls for an outlook more akin to a nomadic hunter than an agrarian gatherer.

9

SELF-DISCIPLINE

"The lack of self-restraint in small matters
will bring ruin to great plans."

– Confucius

My greatest test of self-discipline came as a junior lieutenant on the proving grounds of the Defense Language Institute (DLI) in Monterey, California in the late 1990s. My area studies Master of Arts Program at the Naval Postgraduate School required attaining proficiency in Mandarin Chinese to successfully complete my degree. I finished my coursework and thesis in the first 15 months, then undertook almost 16 months of language training nearby at the Presidio. It was a nerve-wracking time from beginning to end because passing Mandarin came down to only one thing: scoring to baseline requirements on the final reading, listening, and speaking tests at the very end of 64 weeks. Grades in between didn't matter, only insofar as they kept you alive and progressing in the course. Mandarin is rated as one of the most difficult languages to learn at DLI, along with Japanese, Korean, and Arabic.

My study habits in college left much to be desired. I was one of those carefree procrastinators, a classic crammer, preferring the pressure of the moment to force out just-in-time papers. All-nighters were not uncommon at the midpoint and end of each semester in college. This approach would abjectly fail if applied to learning Chinese. We were warned from the start that students not meeting standards would be rolled back to another class, or be removed from school and the military altogether. Some Mandarin students struggled and failed simply because they didn't "have an ear" to distinguish the five different tones in Chinese (flat, rising, falling, dip, neutral). The same pronunciation of characters carries vastly different meanings based solely on the tones.

There were only two officers in our class of 25 and I ended up the class leader based on seniority. That put on a little more pressure—I was supposed to set the example to all these 19–21-year-old enlisted personnel fresh from their basic service-level training. All of them had qualified with high test scores to start Chinese, and I soon found out that most of these airmen, privates, and seamen were brilliant. Their brains absorbed Chinese like a sponge, remembering words on first exposure. The enlisted were energetic quick learners, whereas I was still overcoming language shock and trying to hold on. My sense of trepidation quickly turned to dread.

Classwork took place in a long, low vanilla and brown-painted building erected in the 1920s and 1930s. Large windows opened to a breathtaking view of Monterey Bay. We could hear the sea lions barking in the distance and occasionally even catch of whiff of their pungent odor when the wind blew up the hill.

Our days were filled with six one-hour blocks, intermixed with periodic listening lab sessions. We were taught by a half dozen native Chinese instructors. One male teacher had escaped mainland China during the Cultural Revolution by swimming to Hong Kong. Another female instructor had been a Red Guard in the 1970s but vowed only to share her experiences of those violent and tumultuous times when we were proficient enough to understand her story in Mandarin. Other instructors were native Taiwanese.

For many weeks, we were tested solely on Chinese numbers, each of us with headphones on in cubicles madly scribbling numbers. Every enlisted student would ultimately go to a ship, reconnaissance aircraft, or intelligence center equipped with sophisticated collection capabilities, which required timely mastery of copying numbers spoken in rapid-fire Mandarin, just like on radio calls in the real world.

We were typically done with classwork by 3:00 p.m., but only then did the real work begin. Required self-study, homework, and practicums would consume at least another two to three hours outside of class. Typically, that involved listening to Chinese language tapes over and over again, translating, rewinding, translating. Speaking out loud was essential to improving pronunciation and conversational speed.

For the first time in my life, I was forced to engage in a laborious daily grind. The price for not doing so was immediately exacted—any student who fell behind or did incomplete work would be quickly discovered by the teachers the next day in group reviews. The instructors were not beyond matter-of-fact shaming, expressed in the form of disappointment or faux surprise that a student wasn't performing up to their potential.

Fear of embarrassment, of letting down my instructors, of failing my fellow students, or potentially being washed out of the program created a powerful motivation for me to change my ways. I gradually fell into an orderly study rhythm. This was helped immeasurably by the unavailability of my wife, Lynne, who was also studying Japanese at the time. In the evening, she would listen to her tapes at one end of the house, me on the other end with multiple doors closed between us to avoid an aural clash of our Asian languages.

I also integrated study into my long runs with our dog in the chaparral around Fort Ord, toting a portable tape recorder and listening to Mandarin with earphones. As a visual learner, I created my quick references in pinyin, adding another technique for learning reinforcement by writing my expanding vocabulary down in my preferred format. I also decided to add more language practice by meeting with a Taiwanese student from the Monterey Institute of International Studies.

Yet Mandarin remained a major struggle. Every day was grueling and staying fully committed month after month became an extraordinary test of academic endurance. Every student has their good days and bad days. Sometimes the brain was firing on all synapses and you were in the flow, other times you felt like you were wading waist-deep through language molasses.

The trips to the language labs got progressively more difficult. Our Military Language Instructor, an Air Force master sergeant linguist, seemed to take particular delight in adding artificial static, blips, and frequency interference to our Voice of America transcription exercises.

One student in our class was rolled out and back. The initial enthusiasm of the younger enlisted had started to flag, even though we continued to encourage one another. It gradually became clear that the better students were the ones with more disciplined study habits, not necessarily inherent natural faculties for learning languages.[20]

At last, well over a year later the final exams approached. Everyone's anxiety skyrocketed. Most of these youngsters had never been under such high-stakes pressure. Their careers were on the line. The greatest fear revolved around the oral exams, where each student would face three instructors not from their immediate teaching staff. In whispered conversations, students would say, "As long as I don't get Turbo Wong, I think I might be OK." Teacher Wong, a small, feisty female instructor, had a notorious reputation for interrogating students with a torrent of words, machine-gun style.

Testing began. We took the reading and listening tests as a class, then started rotating individually through interviews. One student broke down and cried in the oral exam, then up-chucked afterward. Others in our class returned wiped out, dazed, mumbling, looking like they'd been run over by a truck.

My turn. I climbed the hill to the testing building, found my assigned room down a long hallway, and opened the door, heart racing. In a small room behind a table sat three female Chinese instructors, steely-eyed and ready for their next victim. Right in the middle sat none other than Turbo Wong! Here we go, I thought to myself, brace for shock. No English from this point on. I prayed it would be one of the good days for the neurons.

Most oral tests last about 35 minutes, enough time for the instructors to determine a student's proficiency with high confidence. Mine was still going after the 45-minute mark. My brain was putty. For the first 15 minutes I answered questions about Spain, where Lynne and I had lived before moving to Monterey. I was asked to compare Spanish and American customs and habits, describe the city where we lived, explain how a bullfight works, and outline the differences between U.S. and Spanish political systems. Next, Turbo Wong launched into a rapid succession of questions on America's strategic approach to Iraq. I caught every fifth word at best but tried to answer based on gisting.

They switched to role-playing, asking me to act as a translator for the DLI Commandant during a visit by a Chinese delegation. I was to oversee introductions, describe the activities of the Chinese departments, academic goals of students, language lab, classroom facilities, and base library. Then it was on to family: they asked me to describe my wife's appearance, personality, and how we met.

I sensed we were finally winding down. Students were advised that every oral exam would usually build to the most difficult questions until you started to falter, and then they would ask a few easy ones at the end. True to form, one of the instructors asked me what I liked to do on the weekends. Relieved it was almost over, I said camping. A second one asked where I like to camp. Easy, I said, Yosemite. After a long pause and with a sly smile, Turbo Wong finished the session by requesting I give her detailed driving directions from Monterey to Yosemite. Sigh! Turbo Wong!!

A few days later we learned our grades. We all needed a 2, 2, 2 score in reading, listening, and speaking. Our instructors were all smiles when they proudly posted the grades. Everyone had passed, reflecting well not just on the students but instructors too. They circled us shaking hands and repeating "gongxi, gongxi" (congratulations). To my surprise, I earned a 2, 3, 2+, the second-highest overall score for the class.

What I learned in those 64 long weeks was that diligence can see you through the hard stuff. Brilliance is great if you have it—I didn't for Mandarin—but discipline always pays dividends. It takes willpower, patience, and self-restraint, but over time all the small commitments can aggregate into something truly special. Wins you will earn, successes you will deserve. As Plato said, "The first and best victory is to conquer self."

> You must first master yourself before you can lead others, which requires self-control.

> Self-discipline is staying true to course regardless of swirling conditions, distractions, pressures, or headwinds that threaten to knock you off center.

> Resist temptations that not only threaten to slow your forward momentum but risk destroying the gains you have earned in life.

> Leaders who go the distance consciously avoid pitfalls and stay doggedly on course in pursuit of worthy goals while steadily accumulating knowledge and life skills.

10

BORN AND BRED

"Progress is not achieved by luck or accident,
but by working on yourself daily."

- Epictetus

As a lieutenant commander with just over 10 years of service in the Navy, I was assigned as the Assistant "N2" for the Seventh Fleet in 2001. That meant I was the second highest-ranking intelligence officer supporting the vice admiral in charge of naval forces in the Western Pacific and most of the Indian Ocean. The Seventh Fleet is comprised of 50–70 ships and submarines, more than 150 aircraft, and over 25,000 sailors operating west of the International Date Line.

Our staff worked on a 30-year-old command ship, USS *Blue Ridge* (LCC-19), homebased in Yokosuka, Japan. The ship was a flat-bottomed amphibious ship that regularly sailed throughout Asia commanding and controlling naval forces responding to developing crises, tracking Chinese, Russian, and North Korean forces, showing the flag, making port calls, exercising, supporting allies, and conducting diplomacy with partners.

The senior intelligence officer was Captain Pete O'Brien, a highly-experienced, charismatic senior leader with a quarter century in the profession. He was a study in contrasts—a silver-haired, muscular workout demon in charge of a profession populated with self-proclaimed nerds, an extrovert leading introverts. He had a personality suitable for a Hollywood actor and a photographic memory fit for a world-class scholar. In one of my first office calls he said, "Mike, my job is across and up. I will be spending the majority of my time advising the admiral and other captains on the staff, which means I need you to run the intelligence team. Listen to your people. Take care of our people. I trust you."

I had led small teams before, but this was my first exposure to leading more than 50 officers and enlisted personnel trying to collect intelligence, conduct rapid all-source analysis, and deliver deep insights into the complex and dynamic geopolitics of the Indo-Pacific region. I was responsible for the day-to-day running of the 24/7/365 intelligence watch teams, tracking operational activity within a 48 million square mile zone, providing indications and warning, monitoring regional tensions, alerting the Fleet on crisis developments, and briefing the admiral and staff. It was an overwhelming amount of responsibility, and I felt the weight of the world on my shoulders.

We faced crisis after crisis. A Chinese fighter pilot notorious for conducting close, unsafe maneuvers around our patrol aircraft collided with a U.S. EP-3 Aries II flying straight and level in international airspace on 1 April 2001. The fighter was almost cut in two by the propellers and the Chinese pilot perished. Heavily damaged, inverted, and plummeting thousands of feet downward, the American pilot finally recovered the patrol aircraft but was forced to execute an emergency landing on Hainan Island in China. The Chinese government held the 24-member American crew hostage for 11 days in an incident that grabbed international headlines and led to a showdown that ultimately took months to resolve.

Violence in other parts of the region threatened lives, economies, and the stability of nation-states ranging from Nepal to Indonesia to the Philippines. We were especially concerned about terrorist threats in the wake of 9/11. The Abu Sayyaf Group (ASG) based out of the southern Philippines kidnapped and murdered foreigners, including Americans. Further west, in December 2001, two

Pakistan-based terrorist groups called Lashkar-e-Taiba (LeT) and Jaish-e-Mohammed (JeM) attacked India's Parliament in New Delhi, killing 12. Strategic tensions rapidly escalated. India and Pakistan halted trade, reduced diplomatic staffs, mobilized their militaries along their long 2,000-plus-mile border, and readied their nuclear forces. It was the closest India and Pakistan came to war since 1971.[21]

We were following threat streams from another terrorist group called Jemaah Islamiyah (JI) that was plotting to kill American sailors on ports of call in Southeast Asia. We were right to be on our guard. Ten months later, JI carried out attacks in Kuta, Bali using car bombs and remotely detonated explosives to attack night clubs frequented by foreigners and the American consulate, killing over 200 people including 88 Australians. A Seventh Fleet staff colleague and his wife, friends of our family who were on leave, had been in the same club the night before.

Later, two North Korean patrol boats opened fire on South Korean patrol boats near the Northern Limit Line in the Yellow Sea. In what became known as the Battle of Yeongpyeong, six South Koreans were killed, and one patrol boat was sunk, while 13 North Koreans were killed.

I had always been a can-do, self-reliant person, and had been promoted to that point largely based on what I had been able to personally lay my hands on. However, dealing with these security challenges while deployed far forward in the Pacific required swallowing my prideful independence and focusing on ensuring our entire intelligence team was prepared to handle the collection, analysis, reporting, and response planning related to these complex situations.

As with all teams, we had a mixture of "wet behind the ears" juniors and older "salty sailors." Early on, I was tempted to simply take charge and organize the intelligence team the way I thought best. After all, I had sufficient positional power and I was pretty confident in my abilities. But Capt. O'Brien's caution to "listen to your people" echoed in my head. Throttling my natural impatience,

I forced myself to slow down. I took the time to solicit input and leaned on others for advice.

I am not a fan of obsessing on process, either talking through it or walking through it, but we jumped in nonetheless. Our officer and enlisted members strategized in multiple meetings about people, positions, workflows, and procedures. It turned out that period of brainstorming was ultimately foundational—not necessarily because of what specifically resulted, but because everyone had a shot at creating the result. The act of simply soliciting views gave people a sense of ownership over our final organizational decisions and laid the groundwork for team loyalty.

Capt. O'Brien monitored our progress and always seemed eerily omniscient about what was happening within the intelligence department. He had his sources and issued on-point guidance wherever needed. His style of artful mentoring involved empowering with a combination of authority and responsibility, providing enough freedom of action for his juniors to learn by doing, and then nudging them with wise, well-timed counsel. Since he was a mesmerizing raconteur, often his lessons came in the form of colorful stories and excerpts from history. He was a master at soft-pedaling his teachings.

We ended up building a mutually supportive team on the flagship characterized by a flat structure (one with minimal hierarchy), transparent communications, off-ship networking skills, and a smart division of labor. Just as Capt. O'Brien had delegated responsibility to me, I, too, discovered the power of delegating to junior officers, chiefs, and petty officers, spreading trust throughout various anchor points on our team and allowing them to mesh their varied talents into a varsity outfit. We max performed at every crisis.

Late one night in the South China Sea, I climbed up a series of ladders in red-lit passageways to catch some air and enjoy the vault of bright stars from the signal bridge, the highest point on the flagship. A silhouette turned to go back inside and respectfully let me have the moment to myself. As we passed, a voice said "How's the greatest intel team in the Navy today, Mike?" It was the three-star admiral and fleet commander posing what came off as a rhetorical question, because he quickly disappeared below before I could answer. The night sky shone particularly bright on the rolling sea that evening.

Both nature and nurture create the finest leaders. No matter one's origin story, no matter one's innate or acquired skills, and no matter what rung one starts out on the leadership ladder, the essential virtue of a maturing leader is genuine humility to keep learning to be a better one. The essential virtue of an accomplished leader is demonstrating magnanimity with knowledge, and an intentional willingness to endow others with insight.

> - We arrive on-station in life with uneven gifts, but all of us have an equal chance to succeed as self-confident, decisive, knowledgeable, team-oriented, and morally driven leaders.
>
> - Even naturally gifted leaders, the minority that displays confidence, magnetism, and interpersonal skills at a young age, must cultivate their innate leadership talent throughout life if they are to become truly successful.
>
> - Progress rests on each individual's openness to undergoing upgrades.
>
> - Leaders are both born and bred, but the best are those who travel through life deeply committed to improving far beyond their start points.

11

SELF-CARE

*"As you grow older, you will discover that you have two hands,
one for helping yourself, the other for helping others."*

– Maya Angelou

I left myself behind and let myself down on more than one occasion, regretting it and paying the price each time.

When I was a lieutenant commander, I was selected to become the first Senior Intelligence Officer for China at the Office of Naval Intelligence (ONI), which involved orchestrating the collection, analysis, production, and delivery of intelligence on China's maritime developments for a 3,000-member organization. It was a tough job to be the "plank owner" of this position, a term that refers to original crewmembers of a newly commissioned ship, especially as a junior officer in a large bureaucracy with natural territorial instincts. In any sizable organization, true integrators are rare. Unless they are repeatedly empowered from the very top, attempts to organize cross-cutting efforts typically run into substantial resistance from middle-level leaders, who tend to be highly protective of their rice bowls.

In this position, I was shuttling back and forth to the Pacific and conducting briefings around Washington on China's submarine programs, more frequent extended-range deployments, anti-ship ballistic missile developments, warship improvements, and other naval advances. I was overseeing a series of simultaneous initiatives, all of them high-visibility projects of deep interest to the Navy staff and Fleet. We faced significant pressure both inside ONI trying to get things done and outside of ONI trying to meet the demand for tailored, relevant, insightful answers for the admiralty. At home, I was also doing my best to help out my wife with nighttime feedings for our second son, Joshua.

On a cold winter day, I was invited to attend the Director of Naval Intelligence's morning update in person before another briefing in the Pentagon, which required me to be in my formal Service Dress Blue uniform. His windowed office overlooked Arlington National Cemetery. After the current intelligence review of key global maritime developments, a staffer listed a series of major intelligence projects in play at the time. After each one, Rear Admiral Porterfield would ask "Who's got lead?" My name popped up three times in a row, and each time all heads turned in my direction for additional commentary on how things were going.

After the meeting adjourned, I walked out of the office with a swell of pride to the anteroom where the admiral's front office executive assistants worked. A number of senior captains, two of whom made admiral in succeeding years, chatted with me on the way out. Suddenly, unexpectedly, I started to feel woozy. My vision collapsed into a narrow tunnel. I took deep breaths to fight back the shrouding, then blacked out, crumpling to the floor. One of the admiral candidates and future Director of Naval Intelligence, Tony Cothron, shook me awake and helped me to my feet. All the senior staff members gathered around in concern. I was horrified. I had fainted in front of everybody, in the very office of our senior community leader. What an impression to leave, how utterly embarrassing. And what a quick trip from a high to a low.

Of course, in my "can do" enthusiasm and "nothing bothers me" attitude, I had underestimated the physical consequences of heavy multitasking, high levels of stress, traveling, skimping on sleep to help take care of an infant, and skipping another breakfast. These things catch up to you. They always do.

Unfortunately, I had to relearn this lesson as a captain. The Chief of Naval Operations (CNO) had dismissed his Director, Commander's Action Group at a critical time as testimony season approached in 2012. I was pulled early from my first commanding officer assignment to help the CNO prepare his written and oral statements for Congress, plus create a variety of supporting references and graphics. We didn't have much time.

Testimony season, which generally occurs in the March-April timeframe, was almost on us. For Service leaders, Combatant Commanders, Agency Directors, Cabinet Secretaries, and many other senior leaders in government, testimony season can be the most visible, high-stakes time of the year. Each official is required to give their version of the State of the Union address to a number of Congressional committees, then answer blistering questions. Many testimony sessions are open, public events under bright lights, televised, with cameras clicking and video recorders blinking red. Hordes of reporters with gallery credentials hunker down in seated or crouched positions at the foot of the semicircular bench reserved for members of Congress. Every seat is filled in the back of the room. All eyes are focused on the official sitting at the long green table.

For many weeks, I worked non-stop with my team, every waking moment absorbed with getting ready. It's an art form to succinctly articulate the Navy's concepts and capabilities, progress in building platforms for the future fleet, readiness levels, long-range shipbuilding plan, and overall sea power strategy. On top of ensuring the accuracy and completeness of our materials, because everything would be submitted for the *Congressional Record,* testimonies need to capture the voice and stylistics of the principal. CNO and I spent significant time in his office, and on the phone in the evening and on weekends crafting his verbiage just so.

We ultimately made our marks and CNO delivered superbly in the limelight of Congress. I would sit behind him during each testimony next to Rear Admiral Craig Faller, who was in charge of legislative affairs for the Navy.[22] We occasionally took questions from the

CNO during the session, which we slipped back and forth to one another on small strips of paper surreptitiously passed under the seats. We would wait for a Senator to start talking when we knew the camera was focused elsewhere. Admiral Faller and I would consult each other, then scribble an answer back for CNO.

Everything turned out swimmingly in the end, but I had not managed a single workout in over eight weeks. The job had become all-consuming. I finally went to my pull-up bar in the house and starting doing a few slow pull-ups. I stopped when I felt a twinge in my right shoulder. On a relatively tame mountain biking ride days later, I went over a small log. The front wheel plunged a couple feet, jerked my arm, and I felt an instant sting of pain. An MRI ultimately revealed a 7-mm tear in my rotator cuff. I didn't sleep well for weeks. Every turn in bed stabbed me awake. It took over a year to recover. Meanwhile, I was not able to run, lift, bike, swim, or sleep right. For too long, I was grumpy and certainly not the best family man or professional at work.

Once again, I had to learn the hard way that self-care is a choice, your own choice. No doubt everyone has to suspend their normal routine at some point to deal with surges at work or home. But extended neglect exacts a heavy price. Giving your all to your mission and your people sounds good on paper, but leaders need to preserve something for themselves to stay effective over the long run.

> Sacrificing for others is an indisputable mark of a real leader, but true leaders also need to manage their own care. Unrelenting self-abnegation always comes at a cost.

> De-conditioning spirals usually manifest mildly at first, but the net result of slow implosion is that leaders no longer operate at peak performance and they are ultimately unable to bring their truly best selves to work.

> Leaders will let others down if they let themselves down. Leaders must be great for their people, but they must be good to themselves as well.

> Leading from the front should not always mean leaving oneself behind.

12

ENTHUSIASM

"Nothing great can be accomplished without enthusiasm."

– Ralph Waldo Emerson

The closest thing to a rock star in the Navy is the Master Chief Petty Officer of the Navy, affectionately known as MCPON (pronounced "mick pawn"). MCPONs are gung ho about the Navy, deeply respected, and uniquely skilled in bringing positivity and high energy to the force. Since 1967, when this position was first established in the Navy, each one has brought a different personality and skill set to bear. Yet all have proven to be master morale boosters across the Navy, single-handedly demonstrating the power and impact of enthusiasm.

MCPON is the senior-most enlisted person in the Service, equivalent to the Sergeant Major of the Army or Chief Master Sergeant of the Air Force. Each MCPON is hand-picked by the Chief of Naval Operations (CNO) and typically serve four years in two sequential two-year terms. They act as an advocate and spokesperson for any enlisted issues up to the highest reaches of the admiralty, ensuring the CNO and other senior leaders are aware and able to take action where appropriate. By protocol, MCPON is treated as the equivalent of a three-star vice admiral.

The MCPON maintains a heavy travel schedule, circuit-riding to sea and shore units, interacting with sailors, listening, learning, and explaining larger Navy goings on. MCPON itineraries are chockful of engagements at every stop, whether inside the country, overseas, or afloat. Visits are periodically interwoven with CNO visits to Fleet concentration areas like Norfolk, San Diego, or Yokosuka, Japan, where the two hold massive town halls together, sharing strategic perspectives, fielding questions, and holding themselves accountable to sailors involved in the high-stakes responsibilities of executing or preparing to execute operations under, over, or on the seas.

A MCPON visit to a unit of any size is a sight to behold. The reverence for the senior-most enlisted leader reflects on every face. Everyone lights up, even the crustiest chiefs. Sailors see someone who has walked in their shoes, who can relate to their challenges, who triumphed over every obstacle. They see someone who is squared away, ship-shape in every respect. Sailors hang on MCPON's every word because they know he will "get real" with them, and tell them like it is, using straightforward language and relatable examples that resonate with the deck plate sailor.

I benefited from MCPON's Midas Touch several times. During my first command in 2011 at the Hopper Information Services Center, a classified information technology command at the Office of Naval Intelligence, I discovered a problem that defied traditional corrective measures. Our chief's mess, a collection of a dozen chief petty officers overseeing hundreds of more junior sailors, was not meshing well as a team. Tension in the ranks due to personality differences radiated down to the junior-most sailor, affecting both the morale and work performance across the board. We tried various fixes, but the problem festered.

Having witnessed MCPON Rick West in action while traveling with him and Admiral Greenert a couple of years earlier, I asked MCPON if he could talk to our chiefs. MCPON not only agreed, he invited all our chiefs to a Surface Navy Association National Symposium, where he was speaking to a crowd of thousands. He then met with them privately to find out how they were doing, what they needed, and how he could help. MCPON West brought his usual high care factor, energy, and trademark enthusiasm. It did the trick, the worm turned. The chiefs returned to the command jazzed up and re-united as a true chief's mess.

Later, in 2023, I invited MCPON James Honea over to the Office of Naval Intelligence when I was the Commander. We didn't have problems to solve this time, but I knew the enterprise would benefit from the fabled MCPON magic, preventative medicine, as it were. True to form, MCPON Honea quickly established a special connection with our sailors, talked candidly, answered queries, spoke passionately, and left a spirited team in his wake.

Everyone brings their own style of leadership to the game. Add genuine enthusiasm to the mix and you start discharging currents of electricity to everyone in transmission distance. Enthusiasm is conveyed through body language, passion in the eyes, tone of voice, or choices of words uttered. You won't need to try hard if the emotion is real. People will know when you are passionate or dispassionate about something. There's a place for both, but expressiveness on matters that count is more likely to win fellow devotees.

> People prefer to follow those who emit a contagious energy about a goal, vision, or dream.

> By pursuing something with all their heart, mind, and soul, leaders inspire and convince others that what they are doing together is truly worthwhile.

> Enthusiastic leaders win support because they exude a passion for what they do and convey a palpable optimism that what can be achieved, will be achieved. Or at least in the striving, that the objective is worth one's best effort.

13

CONSISTENCY?

*"Leaders honor their core values, but they are
flexible in how they execute them."*

– Colin Powell

I learned a lesson in treating every circumstance on its own merits
when I was a White House Fellow from 2005 to 2006. Over a year
as a Fellow, you are invited into the highest levels of government
to meet master practitioners at the top of their game. The amount
of wisdom voluntarily shared by senior officials in all branches of
government is phenomenal. We were reminded by President Bush
on down that "to whom much is given, much is expected." Each
Fellow felt a special obligation to learn and grow as a future leader
of potential.

One evening in the Spring of 2006, all the Fellows were invited
to the Supreme Court for a dinner with a handful of Justices. We sat
on the outside of a large square of long tables in a well-appointed,
spacious room with high ceilings, chandeliers, fireplaces, and wood-
paneled walls bordered with slender Greek columns. Midway through
the dinner, I asked Chief Justice Roberts how often justices changed
their minds about any of the issues before the court.

Justices Roberts, Scalia, and Ginsberg all commented. I had
expected them to explain how their range of conservative, origi-
nalist, textualist, or liberal views guided them to take a position.

Interestingly, they talked about the patience required to truly understand each issue and all its nuances, the importance of legal research performed by the law clerks, the closed-door debates each Justice would have with their teams, and the thoughtfulness required to develop penetrating questions to expose key elements of an oral argument before the bar.

Most surprisingly, Chief Justice Roberts then added "You might think you know what your position will be after all that work, but until you start writing a draft opinion you never really know for sure." He explained that on occasion his arguments simply didn't hang together when attempting to articulate them in written form. The reasoning wouldn't always hold, the position couldn't be adequately defended. In those cases, where the logic wouldn't crystallize after multiple rounds of writing and editing, he found himself compelled to alter his judgment.

Quite a revelation, almost unbelievable. Every Justice was well known to be located somewhere on the liberal, moderate, and conservative scale. They generally hewed to certain well-known judicial philosophies and values. A closer look at Supreme Court Justice's ideological leanings over time, however, suggested not flat lines and perfect consistency, but serrated variance in positions depending on specific cases under review.[23]

The flash of insight was that one can maintain a firm value system and still treat every problem based on its unique attributes. The Justices underscored that any specific judgment should always swing on the specific circumstances in play, which requires maintaining an openness to distinguishing differences and patience to account for contextual divergence. The highest court in the land underscored the importance of maintaining consistency in guiding values, but judging people and their imbroglios based on the merits of each case.

- While leaders should avoid transmitting conflicting signals, consistency has its place. Constancy is critical on fundamental issues like respect for others, character, accountability, values, and ethics, but tailoring solutions for other matters is vital.[24]

- Talented leaders choose varying tactics suitable for each situation. They dial up an approach that will prove most effective for the unique conditions at hand.

- Leadership is about exercising option plays. The same key won't unlock every door. Be consistent on essential principles but learn to change it up where it makes sense.

14

BALANCE

*"We need to do a better job of putting
ourselves on our own 'to do' list."*

– Michelle Obama

I am lucky to have ever been selected as an admiral. As a captain, the traditional path to flag officer candidacy was through a so-called Numbered Fleet position as the top intelligence officer, known in our staff coding as the N2. I was asked by four different admirals to take one of these jobs. I demurred each time, mainly based on family concerns. Refusing top-flight jobs incurs substantial risk in my community because you are signaling that you don't want to be considered for the most competitive, impactful, and rewarding jobs. Saying "no," regardless of the rationale, takes you down a notch, and puts you on the second string.

Yet it was the right thing to do to strike the right balance in my life. I was ordered to become the Third Fleet N2 in San Diego, responsible for the Eastern Pacific and readying strike groups for sea on the west coast. My mother-in-law, however, was suffering from multiple subdural hematomas, and I was not about to leave my wife and family on the East Coast to take care of this medical crisis alone.

Later, I was offered the Fifth Fleet N2 position in Bahrain, but chose a local command position instead, mainly due to the unaccompanied 7,000-mile family separation the Middle East job would require. At the time, the Fifth Fleet N2 was well-known as a king-maker posting, one that greatly enhanced one's chances of being sent to the best follow-on assignments leading to flag officer selection.[25] I admired other officers who made those sacrifices, but I had a wife and two teenage boys who needed me. We adopted both our sons as newborns, maintained open relationships with their birth mothers, and I had vowed to be an active, involved father. That started with being available, not stationed on the other side of the country or overseas for years on end.

So, I did an unheard-of stint of doing six separate jobs in the Washington area as a captain. That provided stability for my boys and kept them among their peer groups in school, the same church youth group, sports teams, and neighborhood friends. I think I did every commute possible, on every radial in the national capital region, driving to tough jobs in Suitland, Ft. Meade, Ft. McNair, Crystal City, and the Pentagon. A small price to pay to maintain the whole-of-life equilibrium for my family.

With careful, long-range planning, I was also able to architect the timing between two jobs. I needed a guaranteed professional sabbatical so I could join my older son, Noah, for a once in a lifetime Boy Scout experience at the Philmont Scout Ranch in Cimarron, New Mexico. I finished up as Director of the Navy's Unmanned Airborne Systems in the summer of 2012 and promptly joined other Scouts and their dads from Troop 1525 for an 11-day, 70-mile hike in the foothills of the Rockies.

Philmont is the Boy Scouts of America's premier High Adventure base, offering 30 staffed camps and 50 trail camps dotted over 200 square miles of rugged terrain ranging from 6,000 to 12,000 feet above sea level. Our Troop had done shakedown hikes for a year in the Shenandoah Valley along sections of the Appalachian Trail to get ready. With heavy packs, we set off into the grandeur of the Philmont trail system. We traversed the wilds, threading forests, crossing streams, walking through the tall grasses in open fields, snaking up switchbacks to mount ridges, taking in nature's flora and fauna in all its raw beauty. The boys would sing lyrics to pop songs now and again. We made camp each night in a different spot, some of them staffed with activities like spar pole climbing, fishing, shooting, archery, horseback riding, roping, and bouldering. One of the funniest things I've seen in my life was a jokey Boy Scout, Michael Dec, who somehow goaded a heifer to footrace him across a field at Crooked Creek. In the evening, usually after supper around the campfire, we would review the day's "roses" (good things), "thorns" (bad things), and "buds" (things to look forward to) as a group of fathers and sons.

Noah and I would break off occasionally to star gaze at night or quietly watch the sunrise from overlooks together before another trek. I was proud of his endurance and positivity throughout the toughest hiking portions, including when he led our party up the last four miles to Comanche Peak and the last day's hike covering 11 miles demanding a climb up to Schaeffer's Pass then across a high ridgeline to the prominent "Tooth of Time." This adventure inspired Noah to stay in scouting until he became an Eagle Scout a couple of years later.

Philmont was an incredible experience for our teenagers and a treasured time for father-son bonding. In retrospect, I realized this break was equally restorative for my own spirits. Too often we forget that humans are highly adaptive, so much so that we can find ourselves inured to drudgery, habituated to a unidimensional existence, perhaps too preoccupied with our professional lives.[26] No one ever strikes a perfect balance for very long, but we are better served when we try to keep the seesaw airborne, which requires regularly pushing off with your feet whenever life overtilts in any one direction.

> A successful life is not simply measured by what you achieve in your profession. Balancing work, intellectual development, family, health, hobbies, friends, and community is essential to your overall vitality.

> Cultivating all aspects of your life will create power centers and sources of strength you can draw on in your times of greatest need. Giving scope to all your talents keeps you on an even keel, washes away stress, and refreshes the spirit.

> Surge when you need to surge but know that persistent imbalances and excesses lead to downfalls sooner or later. Winning at work should not mean losing in life.[27]

> Spread your time and energy across many fronts. Finding the proper symmetry in your life will shape you into a more well-rounded and capable leader— someone others will truly want to emulate.

15

REFLECTION

"Loneliness is the poverty of self; solitude is richness of self."

– May Sarton

The importance of alone time is under-appreciated and notoriously tough to schedule even if you want some. Like many others, I have always found it difficult to resist being completely consumed by the gravitational pulls of work, family, and other routine life functions. It's always one thing after the next. And we live in an age of life interruptus. Interferences persistently crop up, even as we try to keep knocking out our "must-do's." But it's important to secret yourself the gift of time now and again.

In retrospect, I find it amusing the lengths I took to seize slices of private time I knew I needed. During the run-up to the first Gulf War, for example, I had a thorny problem of trying to figure out how to perform pattern analysis of Iraq's military. None of the national intelligence agencies or theater intelligence centers provided the fidelity of tactical level knowledge we needed to understand and predict Iraqi fighter activity, the first line of enemy defenses we might encounter in the pending war. I could find no peace to think through and crack my problem, not in the squadron ready room, aircraft carrier intelligence spaces, or any planning space on the ship.

This went on for days until I finally retreated into a corner of the ship's library. The quiet was vitalizing. I emerged a couple of hours

later with a solution. I realized the only way to have a reliable understanding of enemy air patterns was to manually plot every radar
emission from fighter air intercept radars and every infrared signature associated with fighter jet engine afterburners. We received
those from a variety of offboard sources to a tactical display called
the Joint Operational Tactical System (JOTS). JOTS, however, didn't
have enough computer memory to keep an archive of the intercepts.
The only way to save the data was by preserving the hard copy data
that rolled out of JOTS like cashier receipts.[28]

So, every 24 hours, for months during Desert Shield, I would tear
off the data roll and spend over an hour tediously plotting the previous day's aircraft locations with marker pens on transparency film
overlaid on a map of Iraq. Doing this week after week ultimately gave
me high-quality estimative intelligence that allowed me to establish norms and predict daily flight operations. I knew what types of
fighter aircraft flew where, which day of the week they were active
from each base, which hours they flew during the day, where their
fighter and bombing training ranges existed, and when they would fly
reconnaissance flights on the border between Iraq and Saudi Arabia.
Today, we have machine aids that easily and quickly auto-correlate
this work, but we didn't have those in 1991. Fighter pilots in our
air wing, who would be responsible for fighter sweeps ahead of our
tactical bombing runs, were amazed at the level of detail I was able
to share on enemy air patterns. It gave them a useful intelligence-
derived confidence booster for their planning efforts.

In later deployments as a more senior officer, I learned to find
sanctuary on aircraft carrier sponsons. Sponsons are platform
extensions beyond the outer hull of the ship, below the flight deck,
which host sensors, point defense weapons, and other equipment.
Catwalks connect some of them. Sailors usually have a favored spon-
son, where they go for fresh air and a spot of sunshine. On the USS
Eisenhower (CVN-69), mine was starboard, forward, near catapult
one, with an inspiring view of the carrier's bow dramatically fling-
ing aside the waves at 15–25 knots. Wind in my face, I was able to

better think through challenges, like when the admiral asked me to lead major projects such as developing options for pressurizing or depressurizing Iran, or producing the entire strike group's post-deployment brief.

In shore commands, and more senior positions, I'm embarrassed to admit I fled my assistants to get unbothered think time. In uniform, between meetings, I would slip out and jog up and down flights of stairs. Occasionally I pulled disappearing acts by escaping to bathroom stalls to read something from beginning to end, review points before a talk, or just clear my head. I needed my brain to be firing on all cylinders. You can indeed schedule white space on your calendar, but I learned the hard way it wasn't possible to be at peace until I couldn't be found and knew I couldn't be found.

Carving out moments for yourself can countervail the shallowing of our busy lives. Sometimes, though, you'll have to rage against the machine to get them.

> Undisturbed tranquility provides an opening for constructive engagement with oneself that can lead to breakthroughs.[29]

> Time alone, if used properly, should not be seen as a retreat from life, but a re-energizer, a tonic, a digital detox, an emotional reboot.

> Reflection is where real inspiration comes from. Moments of uninterrupted peace can be the source of powerful ideas, the fount of great initiatives, and the germ of innovation.

16

BOLDNESS

"Be bold, be bold, and everywhere be bold."

– Herbert Spencer

Sometimes being bold is a moral imperative. Sometimes laying it on the line is required when we least feel like doing so.

No intelligence officer likes to be in the public spotlight. For security purposes, we have long been sphinxes guarding our classified city of Thebes. We prefer to do our work in the shadows, quietly and effectively working "behind the green door," content to reap our rewards in heaven.[30] To the vast majority of people in the Intelligence Community, engagement in a public setting offers little profit and teems with danger. It is not just considered risky to accidentally confirm or deny something classified, it's viewed as potentially career-ending.[31] The Intelligence Community traditionally views itself like theater tech folks in black shirts, content to make everything work smoothly from behind the scenes.

The height of boldness in our community is going on public record about anything, and it is considered near suicidal to go deeper than broad generalities on issues of strong public interest, controversy, or, worst of all, political contention. Even principals in charge of intelligence agencies keep a low profile. They are barely known by America and usually only speak at special events. They endure the chore of going on TV when directed by Congress for an open hearing or when tasked by the White House to represent the administration on some-thing they may be best qualified to discuss. Intelligence professionals take extraordinary measures to remain non-partisan and are hyper-alert to keeping their findings free of politicization.

As a one- and two-star admiral, I observed two wildly different approaches to highlighting dangers to our country by senior govern-ment leaders, especially regarding our supposedly number one national security issue of China. In one administration, senior offi-cials sometimes came off as exaggerating the danger of issues like the trade deficit when highlighting the China problem to our country. In another administration, senior officials seemed to prefer prioritiz-ing quiet efforts internal to government and working with allies and partners, rather than spending energy explaining the China prob-lem to America. In terms of educating the nation in open conver-sations, we swung between overheated and undertreated on China. Both Republican and Democratic administrations undertook tough policies on China, and directed actions to strengthen our country and protect ourselves, but by and large most Americans remain only vaguely aware of the full extent of our national and international China challenge. What the country needed was apolitical, honest, continuous, fulsome, calm, balanced, and objective conversations about legitimate high-end dangers to American interests.

In my six years as an admiral, I spent a significant amount of time explaining Chinese matters to others, helping to lubricate wheels whirring inside the government machinery. I conducted what we call "intelligence diplomacy" with other friendly nations as a function of my jobs to talk to other nations' military intelligence officials about shared threats. My bosses encouraged me to do occasional back-grounders with journalists. But I had no public profile addressing China matters, as was befitting our usual intelligence "no see 'em" protocols.

That changed when I was asked as the Commander of the Office of Naval Intelligence to give an open talk at a symposium in San Diego. The Armed Forces Communications and Electronics Association

International and the U.S. Naval Institute were co-hosting their premier sea services Western Conference and Exposition in early 2023. In its 33rd year, the AFCEA West event was a grand networking opportunity that brought together military and industry partners, state-of-the-art maritime technology exhibits, speakers, and the media.

Arriving the day before my speech, I spent hours listening to panels and keynotes. No one was articulating the nature of the China challenge in all its sweeping, ugly forms. I found that irksome and disturbing. Every solution must start by scoping the problem first. Then a lightning bolt struck. That wasn't someone else job, that was my job. I'm the intelligence guy. I'm in the threats and dangers business. That's why I exist, that's why I'm here. It was time to step up and do more.

That night I spent hours completely reworking my notes for the next day's hour-long speaking slot. I had originally intended to talk only about adversary military maritime developments associated with my naval intelligence responsibilities. In the early afternoon, I delivered a much broader, unvetted speech called "An Intelligence Officer's Perspective on China" covering why Americans should care about a wide spectrum of China dangers to our society. I talked about myopia and China blindness. I cast the problem as greater than the Cold War challenge of dealing with the Soviet Union. Connecting wildly differentiated dots to give an integrated perspective on why we needed to get our act together as a country, I appealed for unity and more concerted action to deal with a threat that will affect every American more directly than most appreciated. It was not a speech confined to military matters, it was a comprehensive laydown of our whole-of-society crisis, a quiet dilemma necessitating someone to say "Voldemort," the unspeakable antagonist from the Harry Potter series, out loud.

I expected a slap on the wrist for straying out of my lane, but ex post facto no one in government did so. I received overwhelmingly positive feedback from external audiences after my speech was posted on YouTube. The AFCEA West talk led to invitations to speak in other open forums at the 2023 Sea, Air, Space Symposium on the East Coast, think tanks, and a few universities. The most common feedback I got from average Americans was that they had no idea all that was going on with China. These interactions confirmed my fears that most Americans were sleepwalking on a precipice.

The AFCEA West speech was a step into the unknown for me, especially given the traditional strictures and cultural taboos associated with intelligence. It could have been a firing offense. But the American people deserved to know the truth about dangers to their society.

I realize now that perhaps my journey may have just started in raising alarms to the country. One of my continuing missions now with my uniform off is to sensitize the American public to dangers "inside the wire," in all sectors of our society, from foreign powers that mean us ill will. I must do this, especially if some of our government leaders still think it is not their job to have a conversation with the country about the clear and present dangers before us.

I also need to do my part to help show this nation that their fellow citizen is not their enemy. Americans have a right to understand that the most important struggle for their security, prosperity, and values will not be with their neighbor, but from adversarial states that aim to undermine this country from within and without by any means necessary. If we are to prevail in a strategic competition against modern forces of tyranny, more Americans will need to awaken. And they, too, will need to act more boldly than ever before to deal with the truly paramount realities of our time.

- Leading involves bravery, placing ourselves in situations that demand ascending levels of moral courage.

- How and when to exercise boldness, to act and speak up even when legitimate fears abound, is learned through instinct and trial and error.

- Only through subjecting ourselves to weak-kneed moments do we start to grow increasingly confident and savvy in dealing with danger, whether physical hazards or situational matters like dealing with high-ranking bosses, controversy, or public speaking.

- Doing what you fear overcomes fear. Learn to take risks to grow.

17

PLOWING THROUGH

"He conquers, who endures."

– Persius

I'm a fourth-generation Navy man and I always think about my British grandfather, Hugh Keppel Harry Jeans, and his World War II experiences when I think about enduring adversity and making the best of tough circumstances.

Harry joined the British Merchant Navy as a teenager in the 1930s and transitioned into the Royal Navy after hostilities broke out in 1939. He was assigned submarines and served as an engine room artificer, a highly-skilled enginesmith responsible for maintaining and operating the mechanical power plant. He sailed on numerous war patrols in various S-Class submarines, which were armed with torpedoes, deck and anti-aircraft guns. Each submarine was manned by 48 officers and enlisted sailors, led by a lieutenant captain.

The mortality rate was high for S-Class submarines in World War II. So high, that a song called "Twelve Little S-Boats" was put to a nursery rhyme that recounted the loss of 9 of the 12 submarines that started the war in 1939. My grandfather naturally developed a deep camaraderie with fellow crewmembers undertaking mission after mission around England, the eastern Atlantic, and the Mediterranean. Depth charging by German or Italian merchant escorts and patrol vessels was a common occurrence as the S-Class submarines raided Axis shipping.

Throughout the war, Harry rotated through several submarines. After the first transfer, his former submarine and crew were lost on the next war patrol. Just after reporting to his third S-Class boat, misfortune befell his second submarine as well, with all hands lost on the very next at-sea period. All told, a hundred souls were gone, shipmates, friends, and two Royal Navy families that he had lived in close quarters with for months on end. Harry was devastated and struggled with survivor's guilt. He did not talk about his former lost shipmates for the rest of his life.

The British government produced the motivational poster "Keep Calm and Carry On" in 1939 because they knew its citizens would be subjected to extraordinary hardships and yet needed to stay in the fight. Despite the odds of survival, and like so many others of his generation, Harry lived out the creed and braved over a dozen more war patrols with his third submarine, HMS *Sybil* (P217).

HMS *Sybil* patrolled widely: the North Sea, Bay of Biscay, Tyrrhenian Sea, Aegean Sea, central and eastern Mediterranean, and even as far east as the Strait of Malacca and Singapore near the end of the war.[32] She carried out daring attacks on enemy merchant shipping and engaged in special operations ranging from beach reconnaissance to delivering sabotage materials for the Italian resistance, to landing and extracting French and Greek agents from their war-torn nations. After sinking an Italian merchant off Palermo, Sicily in 1943, Italian escort ships dogged HMS *Sybil* for an entire afternoon dropping 95 depth charges nearby. On the same patrol, the submarine attacked a convoy of three merchant ships and six destroyers, resulting in a counterattack of aerial bombing and depth charging. HMS *Sybil* tangled with a German U-boat, almost ramming it as it dove. After an attack on a German ship off Crete in 1944, the skipper recorded in the ship's log with classic British sangfroid that the submarine chasers' depth charging was "quite accurate."[33]

When forced to persevere through something difficult or scary, I recall my grandfather's ability to endure brushes with death and the foreboding sensation he no doubt felt that fate was nipping at his heels. His experience underscores that the only and best choice sometimes is to hang tough, stay the course, and make the best of a situation when circumstances are out of one's control. But more than that, Harry kept his chin up. He wasn't just stoic but lived for the small moments. He was the guy on the submarine who crafted a metal cribbage board on one patrol and inscribed it with enemy ships with X's through to show the number sunk, which he played often with his mates using broken match sticks for spilikins (pegs). He was the sailor smiling in a black and white picture on liberty in Port Said, Egypt with wavy palm trees in the background. And he was the crewmember who became post-war best friends with a Norwegian resistance agent named Rolph, who Harry bunked with on an infiltration operation near Bergen, Norway in 1942.

Everyone will face some form of adversity. One's forbearance and adaptability—how one consciously chooses to respond to it—make all the difference in how quickly and well one might better hardship.

➤ Any challenge or any job, regardless of how strange, hard, or lost in the doldrums can be converted into a high-learning, productive, impactful experience.

➤ You control your destiny, you are the master of your own fate. Bloom where you are planted. Find sunlight beyond the shadows. Plow through.

➤ Any rough patch can be transformed into a redeeming and worthwhile endeavor. Difficulty is just another opportunity to learn and grow, to make yourself better. One's attitude makes all the difference.

SHAPING
YOUR TEAM

JOINING ALLOYED CHAINS

Leaders handle the highest loads when interconnected with others, linked together in a continuous cross-chain, fit for purpose. Coalescing requires precision fitting, a willingness to open a section of one's own link and settle into another's curves. Just like flash welding in the manufacturing of heavy chains, links gain high integrity through electric currents melting metal at the joints, sealing gaps. Once linked in, being a smooth surface, buckle- and burr-free, allows for the best articulation and freedom of movement along any chain, be it steel or human. Chapters in this section highlight what it takes to operate well as a member of an organization, how to avoid kinking of the team's chain, and what it takes to create all the flush-fitting parts that make an organization ready to take up the heaviest strains.

18

DELEGATING

"Don't be a bottleneck ... force responsibility down and out."

– Donald Rumsfeld

In 1975, at the height of the Cold War, several mid-level naval intelligence professionals discovered a shocking revelation. Pattern analysis of Soviet Navy actions over previous years suggested the USSR possessed advanced knowledge of U.S. Navy force movements and planned exercises. That could mean only one thing—secret communications had been compromised by a spy inside the Navy. The consequences of this breach carried potentially war-winning implications if the U.S. and Soviet Union ever came to blows.

Two of the mid-level intelligence professionals were my father, Bill Studeman, a commander at the time, and Rich Haver, a brilliant civilian analyst. They broke the news to the Director of Naval Intelligence (DNI), Rear Admiral Bobby Inman. Inman trusted the instincts of two of his brightest men, although he was concerned actual evidence of such penetration was scant, circumstantial at best. There was no smoking gun, just peculiar behaviors by the Soviet Navy that suggested they had inside knowledge of U.S. Navy maneuvers. But they had a duty to warn.

Inman delegated the responsibility to Rich Haver to cobble together the story and share their suspicions with the admiralty. Haver was the perfect choice for such a weighty role. He was a tall, imposing figure with a steel-trap mind who could spin a yarn like none other. He also had "street cred" as a former communications and electronic warfare officer flying on EC-121K Constellation and EA-3D Whale intelligence aircraft, one of the largest and most dangerous to ever fly on and off aircraft carriers.

Haver was sent on a round-the-globe briefing circuit to inform the senior most admirals at their stations in every theater. He was empowered by his chain of command and had plenty of moxie to match his powers of articulation. Yet he was repeatedly rebuffed. The three- and four-star admirals demanded more proof. They thought the suspicions were insufficiently compelling. If this intelligence guy was right, the implications would be devastating and require convulsive changes to Navy practices. They weren't ready to roil the Navy based on something so thin.

Haver was rejected at every stop, except his last one in Norfolk. His final brief was to Admiral Isaac Kidd, Commander in Chief of the Atlantic Fleet. Admiral Kidd's father was killed on the bridge of the USS *Arizona* (BB-39) during the Pearl Harbor attack in 1941 while commanding Battleship Division 4. Admiral Kidd listened intently to the brief, then said "You're right. I got a rat someplace in this command." The admiral rose to his feet and walked over to his desk. From a felt-lined oak box, he lifted out a molten piece of gold and cupped it in his hands. "This was scraped off the flag bridge of the *Arizona*," he said solemnly. "If people had listened to intelligence at the time, this isn't all I'd have left of my father."

Fast forward to 1984. Bill Studeman is now Director of Naval Intelligence and Rich Haver his Special Assistant and soon-to-be Deputy Director of Naval Intelligence (DDNI). The Walker spy ring is uncovered. The Navy and FBI learned John Walker, a former Navy warrant officer communications specialist based in Norfolk, had been sharing Top Secret information with the Soviets since 1967. He had recruited his wife, brother, son, and a friend to continue spying after he retired in 1976, allowing the Soviets access to over a million highly classified naval messages.[34]

My father and Haver briefed Secretary of Defense Casper Weinberger and his Senior Military Assistant, Major General Colin Powell, on the terrible news. They walked through the confidentialities of the spy case in the Secretary's spacious office. They shared that the Navy had been warned nine years earlier, but largely ignored it. "How do you know?" said Weinberger. "Well," responded Haver, "because the two of us were the ones trying to warn." Weinberger then commented, "Then you two are the true heroes." Haver shook his head, "No, sir, I don't feel like a hero. My job is not to be right, but to be believed. We didn't have enough evidence. We couldn't convince the Navy to act." After the meeting, on the way out of the door, General Powell rested his hand on Haver's shoulder and observed, "Rich, I've never heard an intelligence officer say that before. You're right, if we don't believe you, you're worthless."[35]

The Secretary of Defense subsequently picked Haver to lead the damage assessment of the Walker case. The delegation was executed with the utmost trust of the cabinet secretary. He authorized Haver to have any access and take whatever steps necessary to determine the extent of the damage to American national security. Haver went on to form a small team of gifted naval intelligence professionals to help him gauge the grievous impact of multiple decades of spying.

Haver ended up being the right person for the job, at the right time. A string of other traitors were discovered within a year of the Walker case. The media labeled 1985 the "Year of the Spy."[36] An appalling number of moles, a dozen total, had been caught stealing and sharing secrets with the Soviets, China, Israel, and other foreign governments from within the CIA, NSA, FBI, and the Navy. Haver's skillfulness in determining the classified findings of the Walker case ultimately led him to be selected to study the intelligence impacts of 43 other espionage cases that broke between the mid-1980s and the mid-1990s. With the help of other talented intelligence experts he personally selected, he managed the damage assessment of the most high-profile ones: Walker/Whitworth, Pollard, Pelton, Larry Wu-Tai Chin, and Ames.

Rich Haver's experiences highlight not just the importance of single-point delegating, carefully picking the ideal person to take on a serious task that might otherwise swamp a senior. It showcases the delicate nature of cascade delegations as other team members need to be brought aboard to help deal with a quandary. Haver's damage assessment responsibilities overlapped with his full-time jobs as Assistant Secretary of Defense for Intelligence Policy, Director of Central Intelligence Deputy for Community Affairs, National Intelligence Officer for Information Operations, and Chief of Staff for the National Intelligence Council.[37]

Haver's success didn't just happen. He had raw talent, to be sure, but leaders at all levels believed in him, opened doors, supported him over the arc of his career. The mentoring and coaching investments he received from notables in the Naval Intelligence community allowed Haver to deepen his expertise and become a powerful leader in his own right. It's worth remembering that if any leader wants ready, capable people in their stable to delegate no-fail projects, they must engage in anticipatory empowering.[38] They must prioritize developing talent in the ranks with an effort on par with other strategic imperatives.

- Leaders moving up the ladder must learn the fine art of load-sharing—not overburdening themselves or their immediate subordinates.

- Seniority comes with accepting that your fate now rests in other's hands, trusting downward, and owning your subordinates' successes and failures.

- Those who achieve the right epiphany pour their every effort into empowering their teams, teaching them necessary skills, sharing hard-won techniques, and giving them every advantage, so subordinates can thrive and excel in their own right.

- Leaders must still discern which select endeavors will require their personal involvement depending on a project's importance, complexity, or sensitivity.

19

AFFECTION

"The quality of affection is what distinguishes superior units."

– James Mattis

F ew things are stronger than bonds between members of a tactical unit who engaged in combat operations. The more intense, uncertain, or violent the experience, the tighter the adhesion. Units that face the "profound existential terror of their mortality"[39] pull together and depend more heavily on one another to help eliminate the danger. They form an iron sense of trust. They develop a group potency that goes beyond normal comradeship as they rise as one to meet pressing military tasks at hand.[40]

Ties like that don't fade. They suspend in time. I know because I've been lucky enough to be associated with my squadron mates since Desert Storm. Our A-6 Intruder squadron name was officially VA-35 Black Panthers, but squadron members still refer to each other as "Rayguns," the call sign used for radio transmissions during our combat deployment.

Our memories of those months leading up to the war and 43 days of fighting from our aircraft carrier in the Red Sea remain crystal. A function of the searing nature of our high-stakes setting. I vividly remember a ready room pep talk by our Executive Officer, Mike "Gunnar" Menth, on the cusp of war that culminated with "Men, the only way home is through Baghdad." That was when it instantly got real for everyone. We each endured the war and its aftereffects in different ways, but the connections to each other long outlasted any hardship.

Our squadron remains in a group e-mail collective and we periodically fire off news of significance to one another. Inside this circle are aircrew from other parent squadrons that augmented us and our Air Wing's former Deputy Air Group Commander, Captain (retired) Dave Park, who flew missions and shared the risks of operating over enemy territory during the war. Our squadron connects with one another religiously each year on the anniversary of the start of Desert Storm, in mid-January, to remember and renew our fellowship. I've only made a few of the in-person reunions, but those who don't manage to make the physical confab sometimes get hilarious group phone or video calls sometime during the evening.

The twentieth anniversary of Desert Storm was particularly special. We met again in Virginia Beach, near Oceana, where our squadron was based. It doesn't matter how mature, experienced, or accomplished any of the squadron members may have become over the years. At a reunion, one's reputation and profile key back to the old days. Good-natured kidding picks up right where it left off. All former quirks, peccadillos, and flubs are publicly and colorfully remembered for the good of the order.

The highlight of the 2011 event was when Bob Wetzel and Jeff Zaun, the pilot and bombardier/navigator shot down and held prisoners for most of the war, recounted their ordeal in every detail to the squadron alumni and wives after dinner. Few of us had heard the whole story in one go, much less together as a squadron family. They each held a beer, stood on either side of a podium, and regaled us for over an hour on their low altitude ejection, escape and evasion attempt, capture, imprisonment, torture, and eventual release. We got two separate takes on the same events, which reflected the unique personality of each of the men. Wild laughter and quiet tears alternately spilled over. It's hard to capture how surreal, cathartic, and curative that golden hour seemed to be.

It delivered closure but also kept an opening to prize something estimable forever.

Group affection borne of trials by fire of any type can be unimaginably strong when personnel are truly motivated to provide altruistic, mutual aid. It's amazing how quickly previous differences lose their power to divide the team when people are united for a common cause. To the extent affection is acknowledged as another intangible but essential attribute of high-performance teams, leaders can help curate esprit de corps no matter the challenges they might face.

> True fraternities are fueled by those who inspirit and encourage one another for common cause.
>
> Platonic affection in the workplace expresses itself in a mutuality that goes beyond just positive regard, compatibility, and team support. It is professional camaraderie routinely manifesting as unqualified volunteerism.
>
> Affection is rooted in trust. It is built on a shared aspiration to serve a transcendent cause. It amalgamates when we believe others are willing to give of themselves without hesitation for the betterment of all. It shows up in every interaction between teammates and its sum is called morale.
>
> History tells us organizations with strong hearts always outperform those equipped only with able minds."

20

MENTORSHIP

"Let us therefore animate and encourage each other."

– George Washington

Mentoring relationships are all around us in different forms, many of them unspoken and unacknowledged. Ralph Waldo Emerson had it right when he said, "In my walks, every man I meet is my superior in some way and in that I learn from him." All of our encounters, including with peers or juniors, offer chances to keep growing if we are suitably attentive and humble enough to take a cue from others. Some people, of course, have more outsized impacts on our lives and the way we think.

I was lucky to have been a student and protégé of Dr. Claude Buss in the last years of his life. I was 29, he was 92. He had been teaching at the Naval Postgraduate School for 20 years before I arrived to start earning my Master's in 1995. Dr. Buss was a venerated figure in the "China Hands" community with deep experience in Asia. He was reputedly the first American to earn a Ph.D. in International Affairs in 1927 before it became a mainstream academic track.

Dr. Buss embarked on a career as a foreign service officer, first in China in the late 1920s and early 1930s. He was serving as the Executive Assistant to the U.S. High Commissioner to the Philippines when Japan invaded in 1942. In the chaos, and as the senior-most remaining State Department official, Dr. Buss was left with the ignoble task of surrendering the U.S. Embassy to the Japanese Imperial Army. He was held as a prisoner of war for almost two years.

After World War II, Dr. Buss taught at Stanford University, the University of Southern California, and the Monterey Institute for International Studies. He authored a half dozen scholarly books on China and Asian affairs, which became standard textbooks for generations of students. He remained a leading voice on the Pacific for decades by continuing to travel throughout the Far East, meeting with foreign officials and other key influencers in the region.

It was clear from the very first that Dr. Buss possessed an inexhaustible enthusiasm for our subject matter. He moved stiffly around the classroom in his favored retro maroon–colored sports jacket, but as soon as he started talking, it was like a quasar lighting off. His intellectual energy would burn brightly for the full two hours. He was intensely interested in student perspectives, exploring how and why we thought the way we did, and used classic Socratic techniques to guide the learning process. Dr. Buss showed unusual deference toward us, even though we were light years his junior and had yet to earn such respect. Only later did we understand how deeply he valued the importance of upholding the dignity of others.

We were in awe of the man. Despite his incredible life experiences and deep knowledge extending back 70 years, he displayed no pretense, no ego, no airs, just a desire to help a new generation of officers think clearly about the Pacific and understand its complex dynamics. Dr. Buss told us we would be the "new practitioners of defense and foreign policy" and much was at stake for us to "get it right."

I'll always remember one particularly important epiphany he delivered my way. We were discussing resistance fighters and collaborators during the Philippine occupation by the Japanese in World War II. I made a pejorative statement about quislings betraying their country. Dr. Buss looked at me and quietly asked, "Lieutenant Studeman, what would you have done in those circumstances? Would you have risked your wife, children, and parent's lives?" I sputtered out some bravado statement. Gently, Dr. Buss coached, "You know, I personally knew many of those families that collaborated with the Japanese. They hated them but tried to make the best of a bad situation. It's easy to think we'd all be heroes, but when faced with life and death choices, not just for yourself, the calculus tends to change." He looked around at the other students, then added, "Collaborators in Manila tried their best to shape the choices of the Japanese occupiers from the inside. Left to their own devices, the Japanese at that time were cruel and merciless. Filipinos working with them tempered many of their worst excesses."

In a flash, history had come alive. Dr. Buss was sharing from firsthand experience, the painful history he lived, highlighting human factors we often overlook in historical and contemporary analysis. I experienced an intellectual jolt, a reset to my presets, and learned a valuable lesson in not judging the world in black-and-white terms.

A year later, at his house in Palo Alto when he was unable to get to the Monterey campus due to medical reasons, Dr. Buss and I talked about tensions in the South China Sea. I was writing my thesis on it.[41] "It doesn't have the stuff of war in it," he said. "But it'll be a contested area replete with low-grade friction and occasional quick flare, short burn crises. Watch, the Chinese will overplay their hand, Mike, and no Southeast Asian nation will ever really trust them. Leaders in Beijing tend to be their own worst enemy." Everything in the last quarter century has proven Dr. Buss right, of course. In the scholarly community, academics say China is the graveyard of prophets, but I knew one oracle whose soothsaying was invariably spot on.

Dr. Buss passed away at 95, just after I graduated. America lost one of its giants. Like many other students whom he made feel special, I was deeply saddened by his loss. He had showered his time and attention on us and I think we all counted him as our mentor.

You might recognize a genuine mentorship relationship only sometime after it's begun, maybe long after. The informal or off-and-on ones can be the most meaningful, the most natural. A mentor can come in all shapes and sizes, at any time in life, and may only emerge when you need them the most. Those relationships usually come when we open to them, and remain humble enough to listen. Mentor-protégé interactions hardly ever end up as closed-loop investments. Those who were protégés usually make better mentors later in life, continuing the cycle of paying it back and paying it forward, benefiting others like ripples extending across a pond.

> Nurturing talent by those above and seeking self-improvement from below should be a standard part of daily dynamics in healthy organizations, where learning and teaching are expected of all.

> Closer professional relationships should not be exercises in coattail riding but rather legitimate access points into more layers of knowledge, offered in the interest of improving how any individual can further contribute to the larger mission and noble cause of a group.

> Genuine, long-lasting mentorships cannot be rushed by either party. Only sincere chemistry between personalities allows both magnets to tug and click.

> One of the key determinants of whether a mentorship relationship ever gets off the ground is whether the senior and the subordinate are both in it for the right reason.

21

COMPETITION

"To collaborative team members, completing one another
is more important than competing with one another."

– John Maxwell

It took me time to realize the truth that team success mattered more than the quality of my singular contributions. For me, it was a slow revelation regarding mutual dependencies with my peers. The dawning began during my second tour in the Navy where I was assigned to a Fleet Ocean Surveillance Facility in Rota, Spain. Our all-source intelligence fusion center shared a building with signals intelligence personnel, which sat in the middle of an "elephant cage" or "bull ring," a circle of tall High Frequency Direction Finding antennas that could intercept long-range communications from its location on the far side of the base airfield.

I was a freshly-minted lieutenant, one of over 20 other junior officers, when I was placed on a 24/7/365 watch responsible for monitoring and reporting any relevant maritime, air, or geopolitical changes in the European theater that might impact naval forces operating in the eastern Atlantic, Barents Sea, North Sea, Baltic Sea, or the Mediterranean. We provided indications and warnings, daily summary reporting, and as-needed radio calls over a top-secret network on any developments that affected maritime units operating in the U.S. Sixth Fleet.

My time in this intelligence command overlapped with the Bosnian War from 1992 to 1995, which followed the dissolution of Yugoslavia after Tito's death. A half dozen constituent republics declared their independence, but extreme nationalists led by Milosevic sought to form a Greater Serbia from chunks of Bosnia and Croatia. It became Europe's deadliest conflict since the end of World War II, marked by genocide, wartime rape, ethnic cleansing, and other crimes against humanity as Serbia attempted to create an ethnically pure state. The majority of victims were Bosnian Muslims.

To limit the influx of more material that could further fuel the Balkans conflict, the U.N. passed a number of Security Resolutions authorizing a naval blockade to stop arms and other war supplies flowing into the Adriatic Sea and on to belligerents. From our watch center, we supported Operation Sharp Guard, which, at any one time, involved 22 ships and eight patrol aircraft supplied by NATO and Western European Union nations, hailing and conducting boarding inspections of thousands of cargo ships bound for the war zone. In capturing violators, this operation marked the first time since 1949 that NATO was involved in wartime operations.

Our watch teams were hard-pressed to keep track of the harrowing blow-by-blow developments in the Balkans war, as well as monitor the Serbian Navy, Air and Air Defense Forces, suspect merchant gun runners, Russian Navy, and dozens of other geopolitical changes in the theater. Each oncoming watch team was successful only when enabled by the off-going watch team. Analysis and research started by one team would transition to the next until done. It didn't matter which team ultimately disseminated the findings—everyone knew the output would reflect the quality of the collective. Experienced and tough lieutenant commanders rode herd over us lieutenants, which created a pseudo foxhole syndrome, where our shared stresses produced mild trauma-induced bonding.

We experienced other co-dependency challenges. Junior officers were sent to the Joint Analysis Center in Molesworth, England to provide naval analytical support for six weeks at a time. We rotated heel-to-toe, relieving a shipmate on those continuous temporary duty stints. We knew our command's reputation and the success of our performance was built on the shoulders and good works of those who had been in the line-up before us. Each of us strove to somehow improve our product quality, processes, and intelligence inputs as we tried to uphold the honor and prestige of our unit before handing over the job to the next colleague.

I had a further taste of selfless teaming at the joint level when assigned for a short period to support the Combined Air Operations Center (CAOC) in Aviano, Italy in early 1994. The CAOC was in charge of Operation Deny Flight, which was designed to prevent any warring party from using the skies over Bosnia as part of the military conflict. I was in the command post early on the morning of February 28 as it calmly dealt with intercepting six Serbian Jastreb (Hawk) J-21 single-seat light attack aircraft that had just conducted a bombing run on a Bosnian factory. I watched the timely and professional collaboration between watch positions, the seamless relay of information, and composed radio calls between the CAOC, airborne early warning aircraft, and coalition fighters. A few minutes later, as authorized, U.S. F-16s shot down four of the Serbian aircraft, damaging a fifth so badly it ultimately crashed before making it back to its Serbian airbase. Those downings represented the first active combat action of NATO in its 45-year existence.[42]

Those early formative experiences taught me the discipline of teaming, lending one's talent for the greater good, and working together to achieve shared goals. Like others in their twenties, I had a stout independent streak. I was known to have a few competitive bones in my body. I certainly wanted to earn my spurs and stand out. However, I came to see that I shined best when my companions also shined. It was more gratifying to enjoy the highs and suffer the lows together, distributing dividends of success and taking edges off any failures, as teammates. You know you have it right when you can genuinely revel in a peer's success because you feel so close to them that you know you've implicitly added to those successes, even if through mere moral support. Competition isn't innately injurious or to be avoided. The key is understanding that the real competition is not the brothers and sisters next to you, but actual opponents and adversaries flying other flags, aiming to do you and others harm.

As you might suspect, many fellow expatriate lieutenants and their spouses from that assignment in Spain became our lifelong family friends.

> Smart executive leaders looking for the best and brightest up-and-comers don't favor dog-eat-dog displays, incessant gladiator battles between employees, or "look at me" tactics. Rather, they actively search for early evidence of extreme maturity, macro-corporate thinking, and promising teaming skills.

> Experienced leaders are more apt to accelerate subordinates who understand that leaders gain power by giving it away (empowering), accrue credibility by crediting others, earn respect by unfailingly demonstrating it, look strong by being honest about weaknesses, and are best *on* the team by being best *for* the team.

> Standing *out* among the competition on the way up a career ladder takes standing *up*, *with*, and *for* your very competition. Seniors know that one "we" is infinitely stronger than a thousand proponents of "me" and will prioritize promotions for people who live out this fundamental truth.

22

ATTENTION

"Could a greater miracle take place than for us to look through each other's eyes for an instant?"

– Henry David Thoreau

I was fortunate to work with Admiral Jon Greenert three times in my career. I supported him as a Special Assistant intermittently in each of his four-star assignments as Commander of U.S. Fleet Forces, Vice Chief of Naval Operations (VCNO), and Chief of Naval Operations (CNO). Admiral Greenert was a certified brainiac, a nuclear submariner by trade who had also mastered the business of financial management, comptrollership, programmatics, and capability integration for the Navy. He possessed a razor-sharp mind. He was incredibly self-disciplined and exacting, but he was also impeccably gracious, amiable, and good-humored. As a Commander, he had earned the prestigious Vice Admiral Stockdale Award for inspirational leadership, a peer-nominated honor.

The first time I met him was at the change of command at U.S. Fleet Forces Command in Norfolk, Virginia. Admiral Greenert relieved Admiral Gary Roughead, a gifted and avuncular leader we all admired, who was moving up to Washington to head the Navy as CNO. Almost 500 staff personnel attended the ceremony in front of the headquarters building. I was one, having been selected by Admiral Roughead to be Director of a new Commander's Initiative

Group, a kind of brain trust cum advisory group helping to advance the fleet commander's priorities.

We all wondered about the new Admiral, especially those of us who were direct reports in the front office. We didn't have to wait long. Admiral Greenert announced from the dais that he wanted to meet each one of us. Sure enough, immediately after the official proceedings, he proceeded right down the ranks shaking every hand, learning names, jobs, hometowns, and favorite football teams. He exchanged a quip or a laugh, making everyone feel seen, special, and connected to their new teammate who just happened to be wearing four stars and occupying the top spot on the flag deck. His personal touch from the very first minute of assuming command became the buzz of the staff and set the tone for the remainder of his tenure in charge of the Fleet.

Years later, Admiral Greenert kindly invited me back onto his senior Navy staff and we worked closely together again, periodically traveling to circulate around our globally-deployed Navy. Often, we would end up executing event after event, usually pressed for time, invariably swimming in sizable groupings of officers, sailors, and civilians. Admiral Greenert once again displayed his patent mindfulness, slowing down to pay attention to every individual, every briefer. He was absorbed in each moment, each interaction—present, available, undistracted, congenial to a fault. He was just as personable in small settings as he was in large ones, giving every event the feel of a fireside chat, whether in a restricted Top Secret update or the middle of an aircraft carrier hangar bay talking with thousands of crewmembers.

Originally, I thought the admiral was demonstrating a special knack for staying focused, but I gradually came to see his approach as voluntary attention-giving. He was living out a leadership fundamental. He was liberally offering his time and his interest. He was giving his undivided attention to people who deserved it because they were doing the substantive, worthy work of the Navy. Admiral Greenert's leadership style included mastery of a simple enough concept—

to be awake in the moment and be at your best with whomever you are with. He showed how it was possible to tame the daily and hourly busyness so that it did not crowd out a leader's basic imperative to bestow quality time on others.

> A leader's constant enemy is distraction, an outgrowth of competing demands and heavy torque on their time.

> A leader must learn to compartmentalize—to become proficient in switching back and forth between topics, ensuring they are present in every moment, engaged at every shift.

> Nothing is more powerful than the "implied flattery of rapt attention."[43] And nothing is so off-putting and trust-reducing as a leader who pretends to hear but is not listening or looks but is not truly trying to see.

> Train yourself in the fine art of paying attention. Give your people unswerving focus, truly listen, and watch unit loyalty, morale, and productivity soar.

23

ENFORCING

"Discipline of others isn't punishment. You discipline to help, to improve, to correct, to prevent, not to punish, humiliate, or retaliate."

– John Wooden

O ne of the stories my family told as I was growing up was about my grandfather on my father's side. "Studie," as he was nicknamed, joined the Army Air Corps in 1930. He entered the Aviation Cadet Pilot Training Program and was shipped off to Brooks Field near San Antonio, Texas. San Antonio had long advertised itself as the starting point on the "Trail of Opportunity" where one could make riches in the oilfields of the southwest or farm on the fertile lands of the Rio Grande Valley. But it was the height of the Depression. Agriculture and ranching industries were struggling, unemployment had skyrocketed, and the homeless swelled shantytowns and flophouses in the cities. Only the Texan oil industry and military bases kept some merchants afloat.

Brooks Field was the home of Primary and Basic Flight Training for the Army. Legendary pilots such as Jimmy Doolittle, Charles Lindbergh, and Claire Chennault had passed through the airfield as either instructors or students at some point. A typical Cadet Pilot would spend 16 months learning to fly in a Consolidated Model 2 PT-3 biplane called the Husky. The training plane lived up to its name.

It was a dog in the sky: slow and underpowered. Its Wright Whirlwind nine-cylinder, air-cooled engine could only propel the airplane to a maximum speed of close to 100 mph; its cruising speed was around 80 mph. The Husky served as the Army's primary training aircraft bridging the World War I-era Curtiss Jennys and Standard J-1s, and the famous PT-13 Stearmans that were first introduced in 1937.

Studie lost a number of buddies during training. Accidents were all too common and the plane was unforgiving if a pilot found himself behind the power curve, turning, and low. From the beginning, pilots were taught emergency procedures and how to select a suitable landing area in case of trouble.

A few months into his training, Cadet Studeman was flying south of the airfield on a navigation flight. His instructor, an Army lieutenant, sat behind him in a tandem configuration providing periodic tips through a Gosport speaking tube, a six-foot rubber tube fed through the instructor's dashboard then into the student's leather helmet. Halfway through the flight, the engine sputtered and coughed and began to lose power. Studie quickly scanned for a spot to set down, lined up for a landing in a broomcorn field, and glided in for a bumpy landing. Before the plane could stop it tore through a barbed wire fence, tangling the undercarriage wheels.

The instructor was livid. One of the cardinal rules for emergency landings was finding a level area free of any major obstacles. Fences could not only destroy biplanes on landing but flip the aircraft and crush the pilots in their open cockpit seats. These weren't theoretical dangers, but lessons written in the blood of other cadets and their instructors.

They had landed close enough to the airfield for a maintenance crew to inspect the engine, fix the configuration, and get it running again. Studie endured the lieutenant's chastisements and then prepared to climb back into the front seat to fly the plane back to the airfield. "Not so fast," said the instructor. He pointed to the fencing debris and ordered Studie to gather up a section. "Into the cockpit with your fencepost, Cadet Studeman," he ordered. Studie struggled to get a broken length of wire-wrapped fencepost into the front seat and also strap himself in. The barbs pricked through his uniform and the wood cramped his leg and arm movements. In great discomfort, he took off and with conspicuous embarrassment, he landed the plane back at Brooks Field, the fencepost protruding from the cockpit for all the other fellow cadets to see.

Studie was ribbed about the incident for the rest of his training, though the story became funnier over time. Not only did he personally learn an unforgettable lesson, how the punishment perfectly "fit the crime" created so much buzz in the squadron that its lessons extended to all the other cadet pilots in training.

Studie's story highlighted more than just the importance of enforcing rules to survive aviating, but the attention any thoughtful teacher should give to tailoring a specific disciplining action so it is suitable and proportional to the error. Much room for creativity exists in this space and should be exercised, both because unique circumstances usually call for it and because the standard set of correctives may simply be inadequate. Turns out, how one assigns penance can maximize the learning value from any given transgression, making it both unforgettable and even appreciated by the transgressor.

How you enforce rules is as important as deciding to act in the first place.

> Always treat those who falter with dignity. Denigrating the guilty party is counterproductive because it threatens to undermine efforts to recapture their loyalty to the organization and the rules that support its operations.[44]

> Be strict without being a tyrant. Be firm without losing one's cool. Learn to distinguish an honest mistake from negligence or willful disobedience.

> Standards exist for a reason. Failure to correct even the smallest infractions can weaken an organization. If you are to lead, you must also learn to enforce.

24

ETHICS

"A man without ethics is a wild beast loosed upon this world."

– Albert Camus

I bore witness to the transition of the old Navy to the new Navy, physically present at the watershed event that forced a major and necessary alteration to the ethical fabric of an entire Service. The tectonic plates shifted in September 1991 at the 35th annual Tailhook Association Symposium in Las Vegas, Nevada. Although it was a forum regularly featuring senior official speakers, professional panels, and trade show-like defense company exhibits, which allowed Navy officers to attend in an official capacity, the event was notorious for its wild atmosphere in the evenings.

Tailhook '91 was the first gathering of Navy and Marine Corps aviators following Desert Storm, which had ended six months earlier. Spirits were running especially high throughout the four-day event, an exuberance stemming from a shared victory in the first major war since Vietnam. Flying in the war was dangerous and many aviators were thrilled to be alive, ready to share their stories and celebrate with their fellow aviators. I was invited by virtue of being in an A-6 Intruder squadron (VA 35) and joined squadron mates on a Navy transport flight out to Nevada. I attended several speeches and remember seeing a Secretary of the Navy for the first time in person as his small entourage toured the convention.

On the third night, Saturday, I wandered from my hotel at Circus Circus to the nearby Las Vegas Hilton, where squadrons had set up hospitality suites along the entire third floor. The pool deck was crowded and crazy as a rock concert. A few girls with their shirts off were cheering as they were being carried on shoulders. The smaller spaces inside were even more raucous and the partying seemed out of control. Alcohol was flowing and people squeezed in and out of hospitality rooms shouting, joking, and checking out the burlesque themes each squadron had set up in their spaces. The more ribald and bawdy, the more crowded the room.

The third-floor hallway itself was unhinged. A buzzing sea of people. It was packed, rowdy, noisy, and claustrophobic. It was hard to maneuver even a few feet without being entangled in someone else. Young aviators ribbed and razzed anyone passing by who interested them. It seemed many individuals of both sexes were touching and being touched, some of it consensually, some of it in a questionable manner. Even as a guy, I felt overwhelmed and uncomfortable. For the first time, I felt what it was like to have my personal space violated at length. I left as soon as I could extricate myself and retired early in my hotel, relieved to regain breathing room.

I later learned that the hallway scene was infamously called the Gauntlet. In the late 1980s, a few aviators began a tradition of slapping their squadron stickers on ladies visiting the third-floor party corridor. When they ran out of stickers, some would pinch or paw. What started as clowning would sometimes go well beyond good-humored horseplay, especially deeper into the night. Tailhook '91 was no different. A number of inebriated men ended up grabbing, groping, and fondling passing women, including a number of female aviators in civilian clothes.

Lieutenant Paula Coughlin, a helicopter pilot and admiral's aide, was one of those women. She was picked up, then knocked to the floor, and manhandled by several men who tore at her clothes, put their hands down her blouse, and tried to remove her underwear. After complaining and receiving lukewarm official support from inside Navy channels, she had the moral courage to go on national TV to tell her story. Congress directed an investigation into the entire scandal. Like many others who attended Tailhook, I was interviewed multiple times. Congress suspended promotions for 4,500 officers, including mine, while the investigation continued. I was a lieutenant junior grade for three years (ensigns and junior grades are normally promoted to the next rank in two-year increments).

At the end of the investigation, 90 people, including a half dozen men, were determined to have been victims of sexual assault. The Secretary of the Navy resigned after accepting responsibility for the incident. The Chief of Naval Operations, Navy Inspector General, Navy Judge Advocate General, and Head of the Naval Investigative Service retired early or moved to less prestigious positions. Over 40 Navy and Marine Corps aviators faced "Admiral's Mast" and were administered non-judicial punishment for conduct unbecoming an officer. Hundreds more found their careers scuttled. The new Secretary, Sean O'Keefe, moved quickly to institute sensitivity training, closed clubs that allowed drinking on Navy bases, and further integrated women into the Service. The status of women in the military was drawn into the national limelight, which ultimately led to decisions by the Secretary of Defense and Congress to allow women to compete for assignments in combat aircraft, crew and command additional classes of ships, and serve in direct combat roles.

Tailhook '91 and its fallout served as an ethical wake-up call for the Navy. The reckoning established a new level of accountability for personnel actions on and off duty. Standards were upgraded or reinforced. The moral components of leadership related to judgment, conduct, and integrity received renewed attention. Secretary O'Keefe described the larger issue as a culture problem, one that had permitted irresponsible and demeaning behavior to exist at too many levels, and he made it clear that those attitudes and behaviors were simply unacceptable.

The Tailhook lesson is that when you don't actively discuss what constitutes principled behavior in your organization, when you don't set boundary conditions, define the moral code, or model ethical behavior, then you can expect Hobbesian forces to take root. Leaders can either consciously head everyone in the right direction or they can let other forces unconsciously aim their people in other directions. It turns out ethical fitness is a year-round team sport, one that swings on the level of honor and discipline instilled in the players by their coaches.

> Leaders are responsible for the ethical fitness of every individual in their charge.

> Organizations that invest in maintaining rigorous standards of accountability erect guardrails for all.

> Perceptions of wrongdoing can be just as harmful as actual violations, so an individual's conduct must always be beyond reproach. When people rise to this calling, they inspirit the assemblages they belong with pride. When people fall short, they betray everyone's confidence in them.

> Right-doing is continually exercising good judgment up a career ladder.[45] Some leaders rising into peak jobs fall victim to something called the Bathsheba syndrome, a hubris-related phenomenon where a senior knowingly crosses ethical red lines, mistakenly believing they now have the power to get away with transgressions.[46] Ignore ethics at your peril.

25

CIVILITY

*"The good of man is the active exercise of his soul's
faculties in conformity with excellence or virtue, or if there
be several human excellences or virtues, in conformity
with the best and most perfect among them."*

– Aristotle

The country would be a better place if it had more citizens like
Steve Murphy. I first met Steve in Norfolk in 2007 when we were
both Commanders. The two of us were in separate sea-going billets
on the waterfront. He was a guided missile destroyer skipper and
I was the senior intelligence officer for a Carrier Strike Group. His
daughter and my youngest son were in first grade together and our
wives befriended one another on the playground.

Steve was tall and lanky in stature, earning him the nickname
"Elbows Murphy" by his basketball teammates in high school. He
was humble and warm, a friend to many, a loving husband, and a
doting father. Steve exuded an aura—a calm, confident presence that
drew you in and put you at ease. He was also "smart as all giddy up,"
as one of his lieutenants once said.

Steve was an academic standout at the U.S. Naval Academy as
well as being part of the Navy Sailing team. Other midshipmen often
turned to him for advice and help, because Steve seemed to have
figured it all out early. Nothing seemed to faze him. Steve went on

to become an accomplished Surface Warfare Officer (or "ship driver") who inspired his crews with discipline and humor. He was fair-minded and a tough coach, telling his junior officers "I am going to challenge you in ways you have not been challenged before."

Unsurprisingly, Steve was selected to be an Olmsted Scholar, a highly competitive program for leadership and cultural immersion. He learned Ukrainian and lived in Kyiv for two years with his wife Carrie. Steve was also a four-time admiral's executive assistant, the latter a mark of someone of immense value to those who shape the Navy.

Loaded with moral fiber and generous of spirit, Steve made you feel like the smartest person in the room, even though he usually was. His combination of brilliance, tenacity, and humility put him on the fast track to become a future flag officer.

I was delighted when I learned in 2011 that he would join the Vice Chief of Naval Operations (VCNO) staff in the Pentagon, where I was assigned as a special assistant and speechwriter. Steve became the deputy executive assistant and we worked closely together on a myriad of projects.

Given his command experience, Steve was hand-picked to be the ghostwriter for a Navy-wide *Charge of Command*, a key document that all prospective commanding officers were obligated to read and sign. In it, officers were reminded that authority, responsibility, and accountability were essential principles at the heart and soul of leadership. Commanding officers were "strictly required to show themselves good examples of honor and virtue." Leaders were counseled to build trust through character, professional competence, judgment, good sense, and respect. Steve added a 1952 quote about a nighttime destroyer collision that killed 176 crewmembers. The excerpt warned that when people "lose the confidence and trust in those who lead, order disintegrates into chaos and purposeful ships into floating derelicts."[47] The *Charge of Command* addressed the timeless qualities of leadership that could apply to any position of high trust, in any walk of life. It was a signature piece of work and could only come from the hand of someone with Steve's character and fine sense of how other human beings should be treated when endowed with authority.

I had a very small office in the back of the admiral's warren. I was later told it was the former VCNOs' toilet many years ago. I would joke that there was still crap coming out of the office. One day, Steve came in and closed the door. "Hey, Steve. This must be serious business if you're shutting the door." Steve gave me a long look, "It is. I wanted you to be the first to know. It looks like I have lymphoma cancer." The words hit me like a freight train. As I looked on in shock, he went on to calmly describe his medical details and treatment plan. Steve's demeanor and reassuring words suggested he cared more about how I was taking it than how he was taking it.

Steve went on to fight his cancer for two years while working part-time for the Chief of Naval Operations and then as a student at the National War College. Between courses of chemotherapy, he helped others navigate their own difficulties, like when a fellow student's wife gave birth to twins three months premature. Steve was the guy who comforted other patients in his hospital while wearing a "Life is Good" t-shirt. According to his chaplain, Steve continued to nurture an authentic spiritual life to the very end. He was "thoughtful, orderly, and buoyant," enduring his own "furnace of affliction," but drawing from it to help others in their most poignant time of need.[48] He walked in grace with his last steps as much as he did his first. On my last visit to see him in the hospital a few weeks before he passed, all he wanted to talk about was my leadership missives to my sailors.

His memorial service in the Naval Academy chapel was a moving celebration of his life. The Chief of Naval Operations, many admirals, shipmates, family, and friends joined to honor what one of his naval aviator colleagues called his "beautiful soul." Steve is probably back in a captain's chair on a bridge wing somewhere in heaven now, sunglasses on, looking out onto his beloved rolling seas, patiently looking forward to being reunited with his loved ones one day.

The world needs more people like Steve Murphy. Steve showed that one can be a squared-away patriot and resolutely pursue worthy causes for country while creating waves of inspiration, respectfulness, and civility in one's wake. He demonstrated what one's best self can look like. Hopefully, his legacy might stir others to try theirs on for size. One can passionately disagree with another, or tackle thorny challenges that demand the utmost of people around us, and still maintain decorum and respect for them. Being civil isn't all that hard. It's simply a matter of choosing a constructive method for making a difference in life.

> Civility centers on behaviors that generate an atmosphere of respect, dignity, and trust.

> Of the many dangers to democracy, one is an abuse of freedom by individuals who feel they have free reign to deprecate others and coarsely foist their absolutist thinking onto an open society. Incivility is a failure of self-control, a form of laziness.

> Americans should remember an underpinning tenet of our nation—that getting ahead requires getting along with one another, not pushing others under the bus. There are many ways to disagree while preserving one another's dignity and respect.

> The price of incivility inside any organization exacts a material cost.[49] The longer misbehavior is allowed to exist, the wider it spreads, and the more expensive it gets.

> Everyone gets to choose what behaviors they will model. Temperate, respectful, and orderly actions create fresh breezes at the backs of others, propelling people to a better place. Recall the wisdom of Teddy Roosevelt: "Order without liberty and liberty without order are equally destructive."

26

FATHOMING

"Leadership must be based on goodwill.
Goodwill does not mean posturing or pandering
to the mob. It means obvious and wholehearted
commitment to helping followers."

– James B. Stockdale

One of the sacred duties of a leader is to help people in their midst succeed in life, not just in their career. Leadership is teachership. It's also about making oneself approachable, being personable enough for people to feel comfortable opening conversations. How the first one goes determines if you'll ever have a second. Sometimes people just need someone to listen, not to judge or fix. The art of fathoming is finding depth in professional relationships, and sounding out one another on the basis of growing trust.

As an example, when I was a lieutenant commander, I had the privilege to get to know a particularly talented junior professional who showed great promise. Intelligence Specialist Third Class (IS3) Josh Devers and I worked together on the Seventh Fleet Staff on USS *Blue Ridge* (LCC-19) stationed in the Far East in 2001.[50] He was calm, grounded, likable, and industrious. Our intelligence team was stronger for his contributions, not just the ones connected to the actual work of maintaining situational awareness and delivering insight on developing events. He was one of the magnetic forces that pulled the team's needle to the true north in terms of fostering a healthy culture, upbeat attitudes, and commitment to mission.

IS3 Devers would occasionally drop into the officer bullpen spaces late at night and we would chat. One night he confided to me he was considering leaving the Navy for other opportunities. I understood. Life in the enlisted ranks is demanding, requiring pluck and resilience, even as it gives options to gain skills and experience in a highly marketable trade. But some are ready and able for more, to graduate to something even more challenging.

I encouraged IS3 to evaluate his personal satisfaction with his current and future prospects, relationships and family situation, life goals and aspirations, and consider well how the Navy did or did not fit into those. I thought he would be successful at whatever he tried, though I offered my view of the power of intelligence in shaping major decisions. I shared that intelligence leaders don't just walk with history, but potentially alter it for the better by helping those in power make more informed choices. One option he could consider was to continue on his current path to complete his degree and then consider a commissioning program to become an officer. He was a superb candidate by any measure and I offered to write him a glowing endorsement.

IS3 stayed with the Navy and ended up promoting quickly through the enlisted ranks. In a follow-on assignment as a First Class Petty Officer, IS1 Devers augmented the Army in Iraq as a Mission Commander for RQ-7B Shadow Unmanned Aerial Vehicles. Shadow drones can fly for seven hours and serve as an eye in the sky, providing aerial reconnaissance, targeting, and battlefield assessment to other forces using a gimbaled imagery camera. As a testament to his leadership, IS1 led peers and superiors, including more senior chief petty officers and junior officer helicopter pilots, in the planning and execution of Shadow missions.

IS1 Devers played an essential role in supporting coalition troops and Joint Special Operations Commanders during a particularly inflamed time in Iraq. It was the spring of 2008, when the cleric

Muqtada al-Sadr's Mahdi Army was engaged in a bloody insurgency along the Euphrates corridor, from southern Iraq to Baghdad. Shia Mahdi militia forces, supported by Special Groups of Iran Quds Force-trained fighters, shelled the Green Zone, engaged in street battles, laid roadside bombs, fought the Iraqi Army for control of eastern Baghdad, and attacked coalition forces with machine guns, mortars, and rocket-propelled grenades. Al-Sadr's forces allowed Shia death squads to assassinate opponents, escalating Shia-Sunni tensions and renewing sectarian violence. IS1 Devers helped Special Operations forces track and remove the worst Shia militant leaders responsible for this bloodshed.

Josh was subsequently selected to be commissioned, becoming what the larger Navy affectionately calls a "mustang," an officer with valuable previous enlisted experience.[51] As an ensign, he led a division of personnel onboard the USS *Kearsarge* (LHD-3), a large-deck amphibious ship with a sizeable shipboard intelligence team. Lieutenant Devers later was assigned as the senior intelligence staff officer (N2) for a Task Force in the Middle East responsible for expeditionary combat forces. Those included naval coastal warfare, naval construction (Seabees), explosive ordnance disposal, expeditionary intelligence, and expeditionary logistics forces. He would soon be embroiled in a short-lived, but highly visible international crisis.

It was January 2016. The captain in charge of Dever's task force ordered a short-notice transit of two riverine command boats from Kuwait to Bahrain. At the time, coalition naval forces were conducting operations in the northern half of the Arabian Gulf. A U.S. and French aircraft carrier were executing periodic flight operations in international waters, which always put Iranian forces on higher alert given the proximity to their littoral territory. Devers knew Iranian Revolutionary Guard Corps small boat forces were provocative and unpredictable at times, prone to aggressive behavior. He advised more time to plan the movement, including thinking through contingencies and arranging additional collection capability to guard during the transit. Instead, the transit was immediately put in motion.

One of the two riverine boats experienced an engineering casualty during the southerly transit. The accompanying boat stopped to help fix the problem, but in the interim, the boats drifted inside the three-nautical mile territorial watermark around Farsi Island, a small but strategically well-positioned Iranian base in the middle of the Arabian Gulf. A number of Iranian small boats intercepted the two U.S. crews and detained them at gunpoint, holding them on Farsi island for 15 hours. Secretary of State John Kerry was forced to call the Iranian Foreign Minister to obtain their release. Embarrassing video footage of American sailors on their knees with their hands on their heads under guard by armed Iranians circulated global news feeds.

In the wake of the incident, all ten crewmembers were reprimanded for deviating from their original course, failing to defend themselves, improperly following Rules of Engagement, and not adhering to the U.S. military Code of Conduct. The squadron and task force commanders were also relieved of command for dereliction of duty. The captain who Devers had advised was deemed negligent in directing an operation "without due regard for mission planning and risk assessment" and disregarding "appropriate backup from his staff." Lt. Devers certainly didn't enjoy witnessing these missteps of history firsthand, but he had done his level best to do the right thing. They should have listened to the mustang.

Devers went on to support cyber operations at the U.S. Tenth Fleet and plans to retire in 2024 after a storied career in the national security arena. His next pursuit is attending a seminary and ultimately leading his faith community on their spiritual journeys, spending his time on another transcendent cause.

Countless other stories like this involve juniors and seniors learning to trust one another, opening opportunities for the transmission of useful counsel, and leading to lives guided onto constructive and rewarding courses. Most of the time, these relationships develop because both parties figure out the benefits of fathoming, acting bravely enough to let down their guard and truly get to know another human being. As Brene Brown teaches, vulnerability is our most accurate measure of courage. When we dare to drop our armor, we open ourselves to experiences that bring purpose and meaning to our lives.[52]

> Understanding the depths of what's transpiring in the lives of people with whom you work involves paying attention to those under your charge, learning about their interests, goals, concerns, and overall well-being. It involves inquisitiveness and asking the right questions at the right time. It involves careful listening and painstaking remembering.

> As you gradually learn about subordinates, you will understand their interests, their family situation, what troubles they may face, what motivates them, and how to tailor your leadership style to bring out the best in them, liberate their hidden talents, and help them succeed.

> All leaders must develop a fingertip feel for their people if they ever hope to become worthy of leading them.

27

DIFFICULT PEOPLE

"As iron sharpens iron, so one man sharpens another."

– Book of Proverbs, Bible

While I was in the throes of completing my master's degree and learning Mandarin, my wife, Lynne, joined me on the Presidio in Monterey. She was authorized to take a foreign language if I was likely to get orders to a country where it could be used. Chances were strong that we might be ordered to a U.S. Navy base in Japan next, so she was able to matriculate into Japanese. Unfortunately, her slated class was canceled, and her only option was to join a class already underway. She was excited to be back in the classroom and figured she could easily catch up on the one week's worth of material she had missed.

Both Chinese and Japanese are considered Level IV languages at the Defense Languge Insitute, the most difficult category given the need to read and write in characters. Japanese requires knowing hiragana, katakana, and kanji. Both languages are formidable to learn, each with its unique challenges. On the Presidio, the Japanese instructors were known to be far stricter than other teachers, including my Chinese instructors. Lynne quickly discovered this to be true.

Lynne arrived as the fifth student in the small class and the only non-active duty member. She introduced herself to the other students as they awaited the teacher's arrival. Upon her entrance, Hiyama sensei walked to the front lectern and stared at Lynne. "Studeman-san, Kyo wa nan gatsu nan nitchi deska?" (Mrs. Studeman, what is today's date and time?). My wife answered smilingly with the only word of Japanese she knew, "Ohio" (good morning). To her surprise, the sensei proceeded to repeat this question again and again, each time more forcibly. As the other students cut apologetic glances at her, Lynne realized she was being subjected to public humiliation for disrupting the flow of the class. From her study of Japanese society, she also knew she would not have been treated this way if I, an active duty officer, had been seated next to her in the classroom. But she was a military spouse without any rank to convey social status.

Four days later, on Friday morning, the weekly quiz was administered. The Japanese instructor explained that this week, unlike the prior, the quiz would be timed. The first week of class with the other students had covered the traditional Japanese alphabet, Hiragana. The second week covered the Westernized alphabet, Katakana. Lynne had tried hard to learn them both at the same time. While her finished work was almost all correct, she just wasn't as fast as the other students and was not able to complete enough of the quiz to earn a passing grade.

At the end of that Friday, she was called into the head teacher's office and told she needed to decide whether or not she was serious about learning Japanese. "When we teach you something, you must learn it immediately. There is no later." The sensei asked Lynne to take the weekend to consider whether or not she was truly interested in the program.

A young army Major graciously offered to study with Lynne over the weekend to try to catch her up. When Lynne described the directive from the head sensei, the Major's mouth dropped open in astonishment. She had been called into the same sensei's office on her first Friday. But the message delivered was quite different: "Patterson Tai, we are worried about your intensity. We want you to know that we do not expect you to learn something the first time it is presented. This class is 16 months long and you must pace yourself."

It was clear in this initial trial by fire that the instructors were setting Lynne up to struggle, wash out, or perhaps quit out of frustration. They underestimated my wife.[53] She met the Japanese instructors' hazing with patience and good cheer. At the end of the first month, Lynne was caught up with the other students, and she and Major Patterson had become fast friends, good-naturedly competing for the top spot in class. Lynne earned the respect of her classmates and instructors, and in short order, they all came to see her as an important addition to both the personality and academic performance of the class.

The lesson here was that we may not be able to control which difficult people enter our lives, but we can certainly control our response to them. It's important to maintain one's composure no matter what kind of crazy is encountered. By exercising patience over time, and taking the moral high ground, behaving well even when others may not, it's possible to shape the behavior of the most challenging people we come in contact with. Accommodating them isn't a sign of weakness, it's a sign of maturity that we haven't given up on their value or their fundamental good nature.

Strong behaviors can become powerful assets if channeled correctly. If not, they can act like kryptonite on any team, exhausting members and weakening group integrity.

Ignoring or pushing difficult people to the fringe is not helpful or even possible. Patiently shaping from the moral high ground can favorably bend relationships.

When it's your boss who's prone to excess, who acts in any extreme, meet it with equal amounts of intense calm. Never underestimate the motive power your boss believes is required to advance the mission.

Few people see themselves as the difficult one, but others may indeed see you in this light. Be willing to accept constructive advice when it comes your way.

28

FORCEFUL BACKUP

"The time is always right to do right."

– Martin Luther King, Jr.

Demonstrating a willingness and faculty to apply forceful backup is essential for leaders at all levels, even in cases where poor decisions may be difficult to reverse. Organizations need independent-minded truth-tellers because groupthink can unconsciously lead people down garden paths toward real trouble. I witnessed such a case in 2002 that led to a controversial international incident, one that was easily avoidable but ultimately required the White House and State Department to smooth over with a key foreign partner.

After a short period of leave in Japan, I returned to the U.S. Seventh Fleet on board USS *Blue Ridge* (LCC-19) to find the staff in a flurry of activity. We had been designated a Joint Task Force (JTF 572) to track and prepare to interdict a North Korean merchant vessel named *So San* that was carrying military cargo to the Middle East. A trio of surface combatants loaded with helicopters and a SEAL platoon was sortied from port and maneuvered to, on order, conduct a maritime interdiction operation. SEALs were experts in opposed visit, board, search, and seizure operations and this operation might meet with hostile resistance from the North Korean crew, who were known to be armed and potentially willing to fight back against a boarding.

We found it challenging to track the *So San* after it departed a North Korean west coast port even though we prioritized national technical means and P-3C patrol aircraft to search the Yellow Sea and likely southbound routes. The North Koreans were very good at operational and communications security, including emissions control from their radios and radars, which made finding them in the open seas along busy merchant routes very difficult. The Seventh Fleet staff and subordinate units were absorbed in these tactical and operational hunting challenges over days and weeks.

I had been mystified from the beginning regarding why we were tasked with this operation. In consulting up the intelligence chain to the Pacific Command J2 staff, the Joint Intelligence Operations Center in Hawaii, and with our staff lawyers, I could find no legitimate rationale for stopping the ship or seizing the ship's cargo. We were confident the shipment contained SCUD surface-to-surface ballistic missiles destined for Yemen. The White House had recently issued a new policy on interdicting shipments of arms capable of carrying weapons of mass destruction (WMD) and the administration was focused on implementing a strategy of preemption to prevent terrorists from acquiring WMD. The President had also proclaimed North Korea, along with Iran and Iraq, formed an "axis of evil." But Yemen was an ally in the global war on terror and there was no indication of a terrorist nexus of any sort with this particular weapons transfer.

A week into the operation I delivered the morning intelligence briefing to the Seventh Fleet Commander, Vice Admiral "Rat" Willard. The admiral was an imposing figure with piercing blue eyes that bore right into you. He was a tenacious F-14 Tomcat pilot, sharp as a tack, and always ready for a brawl. If you had to go to war, he was the admiral you would follow into battle. One of his claims to fame was choreographing dogfights and piloting fighters in the movie Top Gun. The admiral was also intellectually brilliant and more articulate than most intelligence officers I knew. He would run roughshod over staff members who were not prepared to go deep or wide on any topic under discussion.

During the brief, I pointedly described that Yemen had operated SCUD missiles since the 1960s and described how the *So San* shipment of missiles would be incorporated into their order of battle. The admiral caught my drift, stopped me, and asked whether or not the shipment was a legal transfer of military equipment. I said, "Yes sir, this a legitimate state-to-state sale of arms. Neither North Korea nor Yemen are signatories to the Non-Proliferation Treaty or Missile Technology Control Regime. This shipment does not violate any U.N. sanctions and there is no evidence this cargo is bound for terrorists." The admiral's shocked retort was "Then why are we doing this?" This was exactly the question that needed to be asked. The question hung in the air. A pregnant pause...stony silence. It was clear no other staff officers intended to chime in. Having probed quietly into the issue with my contacts on Oahu, I spoke up that the idea had likely developed from the Special Operations Command, Pacific, then socialized with the Pacific Command, which had sold it with the Office of Secretary of Defense and so on higher in government.

Unfortunately, at that point, the operation had so much momentum and support back into the upper reaches of Washington that it continued. The quest to interdict took on a life of its own. The tactical questions of "what to do next" took precedence over the strategic question of "why are we doing this." We were in full flush execution mode. Inertia exercises a powerful force and we were witnessing it in all its ingloriousness.

The Joint Task Force used a number of assets to maintain continual contact on *So San* as it passed through the South China Sea and into the Indian Ocean. One day we noticed the crew painted out the North Korean flag on the exhaust stack (funnel) and disguised the ship's true name on its stern. A foolish mistake since those measures rendered the merchant vessel stateless under international law, which legitimized a boarding where none had been legal up to that point.

In the interests of making this effort a wider, multi-national operation, the U.S. Navy eventually handed off the actual boarding to a Spanish frigate named *Navarra* (F85). The boarding occurred

600 miles southeast of Yemen in the Arabian Sea in early December 2002. At first, the North Korean captain ignored the Spanish ship's direction to stop and the *So San* aggressively maneuvered away from the frigate. It took the Spanish frigate firing warning shots then fast-roping armed Navy and Marine Special Forces from a helicopter onto the merchant ship's deck to take the ship. The inspection revealed 15 SCUB missiles and associated rocket fuel under a thick layer of white cement sacks.

This effort proved to be a successful operational interdiction after a long 6,500-mile journey from North Korea, except now entered the real strategic conundrum. The *So San* crew's decision to anonymize the ship allowed legal boarding, but there was no legal basis for seizing the arms. The Yemeni government officially protested the action and demanded the release of the arms it had contracted and paid for. The incident sparked a state-to-state crisis and generated international headlines. The interdiction threatened to erode Yemen's fragile support for the U.S. and by extension the global war on terror. Yemen was a vital ally at the time given the presence of multiple terrorist organizations operating in ungoverned areas around the Arabian Peninsula.

It took Vice President Cheney calling Yemen's President Saleh and Secretary of State Colin Powell talking to his Yemeni Foreign Minister counterpart to defuse the situation and reduce the bilateral friction. The White House finally issued a statement saying "There is no provision under international law prohibiting Yemen from accepting delivery of missiles from North Korea." The *So San* was released and allowed to unload the SCUD missiles a week later in a Yemeni port.

Although some pundits claimed the *So San* affair showed how serious the U.S. was about stopping proliferation and we demonstrated to Pyongyang the will and ability to stop weapons shipments to suspect clients, the fact of the matter was that the operation was not conceived on a well-established legal basis. There were failures of forceful backup at multiple echelons of command. Even when we arrived at our epiphany on the Seventh Fleet staff that the "why" was unclear, bureaucratic momentum prevented reversing course, resulting in an embarrassing international dilemma.

Forceful backup involves exercising moral courage to prevent mistakes from getting worse. The *So San* case study shows how quickly an oversight can snowball into an ugly mess requiring high-level correctives. Better to speak truth to power early and often to prevent something from growing into crisis proportions. Turns out, it's not just the right thing to do, it's the way to keep doing things right.

> - Forceful backup is the action a subordinate should take when a senior may be edging toward doing something wrong, rash, or unwise.
>
> - If a harmful action has already occurred, bring it to light before a mistake amplifies with time.
>
> - No loyalty should ever be so slavish to any particular individual that it blinds you to condone or participate in behavior that is inappropriate, improper, immoral, or illegal.
>
> - The healthiest organizations foster environments where employees are encouraged to speak truth to power.

29

UNFOULING

"In the middle of difficulty lies opportunity."

– Albert Einstein

I was lucky to be selected to be a commanding officer three times in my Navy career. My first command was the Hopper Information Service Center, one of the major centers subordinate to the Office of Naval Intelligence in Suitland, Maryland. The command was named after Rear Admiral Grace Hopper, who brought the Navy into the computer age. My command was composed of almost 900 people, split between military, civilians, and contractors. Many of the military members were Information Technicians, young and on their first assignment after graduating from their specialized training tracks.

The vast majority of young military members in military intelligence know that they could lose their security clearance by making bad life choices and, therefore, are extremely attentive to following rules on and off duty. People aren't perfect, of course, and poor decisions happen, especially when alcohol is in the mix. One Sunday morning, I received a report from our command master chief, the senior-most enlisted petty officer in the unit, reporting that a young sailor had been stopped for Driving Under the Influence the night before. The Maryland police had breathalyzed him at a sobriety checkpoint. A fellow sailor from the command was also in the car.

The case proceeded to Captain's Mast, a formal proceeding where a commanding officer addresses misconduct in the ranks and issues non-judicial punishment for certain offenses that violate the Uniform Code of Military Justice. Potential punishments for a DUI can range from discharge from service, reduction in pay grade, barring from reenlistment, docked pay, and more. Usually, a commanding officer will not render any judgments until hearing from the accused, the chain of command, and witnesses that might speak on behalf of the member's quality and attributes.

I masted both junior sailors, one after the other, all of us in official white uniforms. The master-at-arms escorted each sailor in before we read out the charges and stepped through the deliberations. To their credit, both sailors owned up to their mistakes, assumed accountability for their actions, and appeared genuinely contrite. Officers and senior enlisted in their workshops attested to their character and performance. But neither sailor had backed one another up on the night of the event and could have hurt or killed others on the road.

After the guilty verdicts, I directed the DUI sailor to a substance abuse program, which is fairly standard in cases like this. I had been in search of a more serious rectification option that carried more gravity. The sailors were worth retaining in service, but I wanted to make sure they truly learned their lesson. I agreed with our leadership team that we should try to inoculate others in the command from making the same heedless decision.

My wife, who had provided thoughtful and creative counsel throughout all of our years in the Navy, suggested I consider sending the sailors to a Mothers Against Drunk Driving (MADD) event. Maybe if they encountered families who had lost loved ones to inebriated motorists, the consequences of their choices might truly sink in. Brilliant.

Six weeks later, the two sailors attended a MADD panel called Resilient Roundtable: Loss of a Child. I added a requirement for the two to back brief the whole command in an All Hands town hall afterward. It was an emotional session. The sailors recounted a mother's tale of losing a young daughter in a drunken hit-and-run. The mother didn't spend much time on the circumstances of the accident, though. She described her daughter: her personality, the songs she liked to sing, the kind of pictures she drew for her family, what she wanted to be when she grew up, and the mother's favorite small little moments with her daughter. The sailors choked up as they talked. You could have heard a pin drop when they were done. Hundreds of eyes in the room glistened with tears. I shook the sailors' hands and whispered "That was brave."

It was a fencepost-in-cockpit moment. A narrow lesson widened to educate a broader audience through an indelible emotive sting. Needless to say, we didn't have another DUI. Those two sailors earned back the respect of their shipmates and proved to be solid performers for the remainder of their tour and beyond. Their courage to face the music and the way they made amends for their misjudgment became a testament to their honor and professionalism. Their pathway back to finding rectification also radiated an important lesson throughout the entire organization.

> A vast majority of mistakes are innocent, tolerable, and simply part of our individual and collective learning processes. Leaders at all levels must provide an environment where efforts to learn and contribute are prized and rewarded, and a high tolerance should exist for pitfalls and stumbles along the way.

> Honest mistakes should be tolerated, but lapses in character or integrity will be less easily forgiven.

> Dodging blame for any wrongdoing is a sign of immaturity and unprofessionalism, a signal that someone is not ready to take accountability for their actions or those who work for them.

> If handled the right way, how you respond to a failure, and the way you unfoul line and anchor can re-inspire people's faith and trust in your capabilities, character, and professionalism.

30
ASSERTIVENESS

"Fortune favors the bold."

- Virgil

Cathy Johnston's picture should be next to the word "assertive" in the dictionary. You would see a petite blonde with bobbed hair with bright, confident eyes ready to take on the world. Cathy has applied her spirited energy against our toughest security problems. I've heard others affectionately describe her as a badass, a force of nature, and a whirlwind of enthusiasm. She consistently demonstrated how to glide over institutional fences that would stop others dead in their tracks. Cathy was so effective that she was handed some of the most important jobs in Defense Intelligence and was properly elevated to a high Senior Executive Service rank.

The span of my career overlapped with Cathy's and I was better for it. We first met when she was a Senior Defense Expert for China and East Asia at the Defense Intelligence Agency (DIA) in the late 1990s. She was uniquely qualified for this role. She was born in Taiwan and spent 13 years growing up in Asia before attending Princeton University, where she competed as a gymnast. She also had a master's degree in Chinese Studies and spoke Mandarin. In our collaboration on a series of projects, I saw her drive forward as a powerful difference-maker. Her technique to overcome bureaucratic sludginess was to win people over with her passion, vivacity, and raw intellect. On top of everything else, she was a mother of two, an accomplished lyric soprano, and an amateur triathlete. I've encountered few people who could keep up with Cathy.

Cathy was adept at crossing into whatever lanes got the business of the nation done. As DIA's Director of Analysis, she worked across the defense intelligence enterprise developing new approaches to all-source analysis. At the Central Intelligence Agency, she worked with a variety of partners to field innovative technical solutions to collecting on what we called "hard targets." At the Office of the Director of National Intelligence, she served as a principal deputy overseeing Intelligence Community-wide requirements and resource investments that totaled billions of dollars. She was also the first National Intelligence Manager for East Asia, in charge of choreographing improved collection and analysis on an inscrutable China and the hermit kingdom of North Korea for the Director of National Intelligence. Cathy's network of teammates from across the U.S. and allied national security field could fill scores of rolodexes of old.

Cathy always seeks positions where she can have the greatest impact, so I was not surprised when she called me up when I was the Southern Command Director of Intelligence (J2) to inquire about tips on interviewing for a Deputy J2 job opening at the Indo-Pacific Command. She got the job. In a remarkable twist of fate, a short time later I was asked to do two Combatant Command J2 stints in a row, a rare occurrence at the time, and I showed up in Oahu a couple of months after her. Drawing on our long-established trust and mutual respect, we tag-teamed for three years, vigorously advancing our intelligence contributions in the theater. We became somewhat of a dynamic duo. I couldn't have asked for a more perfect professional partner. I considered Cathy a co-J2, not just a Deputy.

Cathy's charge-ahead assertiveness broke through the red tape and dillydallying we too frequently encountered. The standard protocol for principal-to-principal coordination in the government, for instance, was for aides to set up a call or videophone session, and the staff would find a convenient time in the next few hours or days to discuss a subject. Cathy was a famous lightning cold-caller. It didn't matter who it was, or how senior they were, if we needed to warn, inform, or resolve something, she immediately patched through, pleasantly and insistently pressed forward, and took care of business. Her style was so winning, her pep so infectious, people were amped to help. The call was probably the highlight of their day. She was like Neo in the Matrix movies long after he swallowed the red pill. She altered physics to make bureaucracies dance when they otherwise tended to default to their fixed positions as blue-pilled wallflowers.

Her assertiveness played a swing role as we reviewed proposals for military operations in the Indo-Pacific. Whether at planning sessions among captains and colonels, general and flag officer screenings, or four-star leader update sessions, she pulled no punches when it came to evaluating the risks, potential unintended consequences, and likely efficacy of a particular intended movement of ships, aircraft, or special forces. Intelligence professionals can sometimes become shrinking violets when involved in contentious debates on the best use of the military instrument. Most are excellent on the well-rehearsed first-round offering of intelligence inputs, but only the very best kick around options and alternatives with seniors until the very end, putting their credibility and stock on the line, if needed, to dissuade a commander of something unwise. Cathy wasn't a two-dimensional intelligence officer bounded by billet, she was a three-dimensional solutions-finder immersed with other mission-focused staff members, habitually going above and beyond what was outlined in her job description to help formulate what to do about the intelligence we provided.

Her patented assertiveness was also an asset during high-stakes meetings with senior Defense officials, Congressmen, and Intelligence Agency leaders. In principal's sessions, the normal protocol is to wait until your boss invites you to comment on something requiring expert intelligence input. Cathy would launch a well-timed zinger comment whenever the conversation deserved a logic or knowledge check. Every organization needs its Cathys.

It turns out one's influence is directly proportional not only to one's accumulated expertise and ability to apply it but the backbone to inject value wherever one can add it. Sometimes that means going outside one's swim lane to move things along for the collective. All the best leaders I've known have given their people the freedom of action to contribute beyond their specialty, and rewarded them for it, so long as it conformed to overarching guidance, placed mission above self, and catalyzed higher team performance. Orchestrating an organization isn't just about collecting the finest instruments for sheet music reading, it's allowing the band to engage in a bit of jazz improv. In any organization, room must be left for the most confident and talented people to assert themselves beyond the typical limit lines, wherever and whenever it counts, to elevate group gameplay.

> Ingenius leaders find ways to influence outcomes on issues over which they have no authority.[54]

> Being eager to contribute to matters beyond your immediate job responsibilities strengthens organizational meshing and improves decision-making across an enterprise.[55]

> Every bit of knowledge, every added experience, and every new way that you expose yourself will help prepare you for increased responsibilities down the road.

> Assertive individuals, those who initiate smart actions to further the organization regardless of their title or position, are often an outfit's most highly prized assets.[56]

31

FOCUS

"If there is any one 'secret' of effectiveness, it is concentration. Effective executives do first things first and they do one thing at a time."

– Peter Drucker

One strategic weakness of especially large organizations is their tendency to fragment into specialized areas and grow apart from one another. The left and the right hands float away, fingers and toes separate. Opportunities to commune diminish. People stick to their corners, fight their own fires, and manage parochial tasks. Even where there may still be an overarching vision and shared sense of purpose, the natural outflow of daily activity branches people into their tributaries. Rivers of tasking often force people to struggle just to keep their heads above white water. As a result, enterprise team integrity can suffer. And myopia can become a major liability.

As the new Commander of the Office of Naval Intelligence (ONI) in 2022, I knew my organization faced this problem of institutional drift. We also faced a crisis of intellectual compression. ONI had perfected creating cylinders of excellence. We historically valued hyper expertise and deep knowledge. We were famous for it. The problem was we didn't value enough breadth in the mix. It grew by happenstance, based on an individual's choice to diversify. It was not systemically cultivated to the degree required, so we had too few people with broad enough experience within our enterprise. We desperately needed more versatility in the ranks, analysts and supervisors who were masters in connecting the dots, capable of seeing across boundary layers, and able to serve as true integrators of intelligence. We needed more people in possession of a synoptic view of our adversaries.

One of the many ways our leadership team tackled these twin issues of disintegration and bureaucratic narrowing was to create a forum for regular group learning. We called it Knowledge 360 or K360. Twice a week, every week, for an hour, we would arrange speakers to present Technology, Entertainment, and Design (TED)-like presentations in our main auditorium. These were live-streamed and archived on our intranet. The intent was to dedicate predictable windows of time for learning, to promote cross-pollination. We opened opportunities for thousands of people from within the enterprise to associate with one another. We entered into a rhythm of sharing tailored knowledge at scale with the workforce.

One of our best female Navy captains led the orchestration of it all. I would attend as many of the sessions as possible, knowing it might bring in more attendees. The question and answer period occasionally led to an evaluation of how certain new insights might be applied within our headquarters. Speakers included former and current senior government officials, think tank experts, famous authors, academics, technologists, and other Intelligence Community experts. Some of our best sessions were unclassified ones where informed authorities filled gaps and rounded out what we knew through classified channels.

As importantly, we interleaved ONI's experts into the line-up. For many, it was the first time they finally figured out what some-one just down the hall from them was contributing to the mission. They didn't just learn new things, they had a face and a name to initiate contact for work on related projects. Speakers, of course, received immediate positive feedback, a boost to their credibility, and a burnished reputation. The corporate visibility of the K360 sessions made them feel their work was significantly more valued.

Looking back, I also saw the importance of the team spending time absorbed in just one thing at a time. Desk work for many is all train station hubbub. People just can't find sanctuary from the frenzy. Employees appreciated the sanction to cut away, physically extricate themselves from their buzzing cockpits, and go to a place where they could dwell on a single topic for an extended period of time. They could learn by directly interacting with a subject matter expert. They could deeply immerse. They could think without distraction. For many, a particular K360 could be the highlight of their week. People enjoyed the sensation of being invested with new knowledge and having a chance to submerge into all the layers.

Both leaders and subordinates can overestimate their ability to multi-task without penalty. The price is more insidious than we'd like to admit. It is worth re-teaching ourselves how to single-task, to focus on one thing, and one thing only for the duration that one thing deserves. Whether leaders want their teams to absorb high-quality inputs or deliver high-quality outputs, success can often hinge on allowing them uninterrupted blocks of time to do either.

> Performing in a constant state of fragmentation keeps the brain in the shallows. A mental tax is exacted every time the mind has to reorient itself and the price for repeatedly breaking concentration is chronic scatter-braining.[57]

> Some projects require long stretches of concentrated effort, an undisturbed block of time in deep immersion to make real progress.[58]

> Know how to juggle, but also schedule fenced-off, imaginative, and critical thinking time to focus in-depth on things that count.

> The most successful employees know everything about some things and something about everything.

32

COUNSELING

"The mind is not a vessel to be filled, but a fire to be kindled."

– Plutarch

As an officer, I always tried to take counseling to others seriously, because throughout my career few took it seriously enough with me. Often, I would just receive encouragement to keep doing what I was doing when what I craved was constructive criticism that allowed me to work on my defects. I knew I had plenty, I just wanted to know which ones were the most egregious or obvious to others, which ones were getting in the way of becoming a better leader, a better human.

The best critique I ever received was from the Director of the White House Fellow program, Janet Eissenstat, who told me early in the program in 2005, "Mike, you need to polish up your first impressions. You come off as too wary and standoffish. Establish an instant connection. Work on your warmth." I was so thrilled and appreciative to hear this brutally honest remark that Janet probably thought I was a weirdo. She walked away from me as I continued to grin and nod my head.

Counseling well takes guts. The senior has to take the risk of potentially offending the junior. Sensitivities run so high during some counseling sessions that both parties often beat around the bush, talk in code, hover in generalities, and hope one another will pick up on some subtle hint buried deep inside a particular platitude. They check the box, breathe a sigh of relief, and move on. This timorous approach does a distinct disservice to everyone. Counseling should be a time for plain-spokenness, a chance to coach one-on-one, and an opportunity to offer course corrections to improve individual and ultimately team performance. Counseling done wrong is rushed, perfunctory business. Counseling done right dwells in the discomfort but enters and leaves it smoothly with professionalism and mutual respect.

Most organizations follow some type of regimented counseling formula. The most important counseling sessions, though, can be ad hoc ones, necessitated by fluid circumstances. When I was Director of Intelligence at Indo-Pacific Command, for instance, I grew concerned my new executive assistant, a field grade officer, seemed troubled. He was sharp, well-organized, a people person. He possessed all the perfect attributes to thrive in a flag officer front office and fast-moving joint command. He ran a tight ship, completed tasks ahead of time, and successfully juggled dozens of glass balls, none of which we could afford to drop. But something nagged.

We met multiple times and I inquired how things were going, taking our time to let our conversations simmer. Our rapport was good and he knew I cared. The officer eventually shared more personal information with me, so I knew he was dealing with out-of-office challenges, but overall he insisted everything was manageable. By month four into his tenure, though, I sensed the mood had palpably shifted in the front office. Any one person can affect front-office chemistry because those teams are so tight-knit. Anxiety can be contagious. Tasks were still being completed, but our mojo was off. Where we had worked hard, but lightheartedly before, everyone now seemed to be walking around on tenterhooks.

Finally, late on a Friday, I invited him into the office for a private chat. I expressed my concerns about his situation, especially the multiple simultaneous life events he was facing, including taking care of an infant child and dealing with an incident that carried over from a previous assignment. I put it right out there, "Are you happy?" He looked me in the eye and quietly said "No." "Then why don't we do something about it," I replied softly. "Listen, I know you're supposed to tough it out for a least a year in this job, but if it's not working out for you, if you've got too much going on, let's just call a spade a spade and make an adjustment." I told him that he shouldn't worry about his fitness report paperwork and that I would give him strong marks. But I wanted him to talk with his wife over the weekend and tell me on Monday what he had decided. Monday rolled around. He walked in a different man like a weight had been lifted off his shoulders. "OK, sir, I've decided to transition to another job with less intensity. Thank you for all your support. It means a lot." *Voila.* We found our win-win.

Part of a leader's job is to not let their people suffer *in* silence, or let their team suffer *from* silence. Words unsaid, questions unasked, and issues left unbroached will only leave ticking time bombs hidden just under the surface of an organization. While supervisors might rationalize that they are being polite by avoiding sticky personnel issues or saving a subordinate's "face," all they are doing is denying an employee the professional courtesy they are due. Even worse, they are choosing to abrogate their duty to listen and responsibly coach. In counseling, candor is the coin of the realm. Employees deserve to know where they stand. They merit thoughtful, personalized advice on where to improve. And they have a right to be presented with openings to share whatever matters are on their minds. If leaders don't give breathing room for these things, they should expect unvented steam to start bursting the seams of their organization's boiler.

> Employees deserve to know where they stand and how well they are living up to standards, expectations, and performance objectives.

> The longer you wait to address performance shortfalls, the more ingrained poor habits will become; the longer you wait to praise good deeds, the less powerful the reinforcement of positive behavior.

> Listen and talk out issues together, so you can better understand one another's perspective.[59] Share candid advice to nourish talent.

> Providing active feedback is a sign that you genuinely care about individual growth and team success. It's another way to build tungsten strength into an organization.

33

LATITUDE

*"Leading is more about being part of a feedback loop within a
system than it is about being at the top of a command chain."*

– Stanley McChrystal

As a special assistant, my favorite stop to arrange for the Chief
of Naval Operations (CNO), Admiral Greenert, was to see his
junior trailblazers in Norfolk. The admiral had the foresight to establish a cohort of non-establishment thinkers within a new CNO Rapid
Innovation Cell (CRIC), which ran from 2012 to 2016. The CRIC was
composed of a rotating group of 12–15 junior officers and enlisted,
none of them above the rank of lieutenant commander, who maintained their full-time jobs but collaborated in a matrixed way on
diverse projects. New CRIC members were selected by the junior
circle and could only join if they offered a radical idea that could solve
a noteworthy naval problem.

The CNO funneled resources to help support this "safe house for
disruptive thinking" and develop the ideas of these bright young individuals.[60] He also facilitated introductions with other government
and industry leaders and encouraged them to explore commercial
sector technology that could apply to the Navy. CNO was comfortable
with the "fail early, fail often" experimentation so long as creative
solutions kept coming. After all, the CNO specifically engineered the
CRIC to amplify the institutionally weaker voices across the Navy.

He knew talented junior pioneers had much to offer and the CRIC would create a direct channel to the top of the Navy. It made no sense to him to let juniors sit on their ideas for years, simply waiting until they earned enough seniority to act on them.

At each quarterly meeting in person with the CNO, the entrepreneurial CRIC members would run through their projects. Each was a champion for early adoption of various technologies and described how they could benefit the Navy. The sessions had a Shark Tank feel, but were safer, because the CNO was already inclined to give seed money. One officer described the benefits of afloat additive manufacturing, or 3-D printing, where ships could print replacement engineering or aircraft parts based on e-mailed designs. Another showcased how augmented reality using technology like Google Glass could help maintenance personnel run through checklists using eyeglasses with interactive head-up displays. A young officer showed a video experimenting with biomimetics, in this case, a stealthy unmanned underwater vehicle shaped and propelled like a large tuna fish. An articulate petty officer proposed a personal mobile application for sailors similar to LinkedIn, which would allow their qualification profiles to be matched with prospective job openings in the Navy for improved transparency and assignment negotiability. There was even a renewable energy proposal to demo at the U.S. Naval Academy for an anaerobic digestion process that could convert tons of midshipmen galley food waste to methane and then electricity.

Dozens of these projects ended up being fielded in various ways across the Navy. The CRIC successes helped inspire Secretary of the Navy Ray Mabus to establish a more expansive Task Force Innovation in 2015, which helped to stimulate additional ideas and accelerate opportunities through rapid identification and funding of promising small projects for wider adoption across the Navy Department.

The Navy owes much to the young pathfinders at the CRIC. Elements of today's modernized personnel management system, its so-called "Ready, Relevant Learning" approach, and initiatives like the NavalX innovation and agility cell that bridges the military, academia, and commercial sectors, can trace their evolution back to the burst of ideas first shepherded forward through the CRIC concept.

Every organization has to figure out how they'll "let a hundred flowers bloom, and a hundred schools of thought contend."[61] Brilliant ideas can come from any quarter, at any time. The onus is on leaders to best architect an environment so ideas are freely and perpetually volunteered and their brainchildren duly rewarded. It's about engineering a culture that encourages latitude for people and then listens to the people who exercise that latitude. Invariably it takes active solicitation, not passive hope, however, to endow people with the psychological safety they usually need to open up.

> Any sizable organization needs hierarchy, disciplined processes, and established protocols, but authority and subordination do not mean individuals must become leaden, inert components of a labyrinthine bureaucracy.

> Leaders must help their people move beyond learned rigidities that can stifle freedom of thought and inquiry. People must be given enough scope to truly flourish.

> Our strategic advantage as a nation has always been in our pluralism and diversity. We are stronger because we widely disperse decision-making points and trust our people.

> Organizations that enfranchise, empower, and enable their people will always outcompete their competitors so long as they continue to mobilize the brainpower of those down and across the ranks.

34

CLIMATE

"The moral climate of any organization, larger than that of the individual, is created hour by hour through the multitude of choices and behaviors of its members."

– Rushworth Kidder

Whether at the macro or micro levels, in a large ecosystem, or a small organization of any type, people seem to constantly relearn Plutarch's lesson that "the richest soil, if left uncultivated, produces the rankest weeds." What happens in substratum layers around us is hard to fully understand, but left to the vagaries of natural forces, we know entropy usually takes over. Proactive climate shaping can prevent a decline into disorder, though sometimes it's hard to know how much energy should be applied in this area.

The world watched this phenomenon play out on a global scale as different factions in the Muslim world contended for the soul of Islam. The rise of Islamic extremism, particularly since the late 1990s, was abetted by strong, spirited voices calling for jihad not just in the Middle East, but worldwide. Through the use of extensive propaganda on multiple social media platforms, appealing to disaffected youth and other sympathizers, including many well-educated Muslims, a relatively small minority of Muslims successfully radicalized tens of thousands of followers to commit heinous acts in the name of Allah. The 9/11 attacks prompted the so-called Global War on Terror, which defined the first decades of the 21st century.

A key question for many years has been where the moderate voices on Islam have been, and why weren't they more active in minimizing the appeal of zealots. At the National War College in 2015, I went to Egypt with a dozen fellow students to get answers to this question. We were hosted by the Egyptian military, which provided access to a fulsome learning experience.

In the blazing heat, we were taken back and forth across Cairo for engagements at the 1973 October War Museum, Egyptian Command and Staff College, and the Egyptian Council on Foreign Affairs. Early on, our hosts also took us under armed escort for an obligatory visit to Ishmailia to tour the Canal Zone and hear from the Director of the Suez Canal Authority. In one of the most surreal moments of my career, as the senior officer in the group and the only Navy guy, I was invited to pilot Anwar Sadat's old Presidential yacht between sand dunes during an on-water tour of the canal as gigantic container ships motored by 100 feet away in a northbound convoy.

The most enlightening stop was a rare audience with the Grand Sheikh, aka Grand Imam of al-Azhar, Ahmed el-Tayeb. The al-Azhar is the second oldest university in the world, which has provided teachings continuously since 975 CE. In the Sunni Muslim world, the Imam is the highest authority on Islamic jurisprudence. The Grand Imam had studied at the University of Paris, held a Ph.D. in Islamic Philosophy, and had taught at universities in Saudi Arabia, Qatar, and the United Arab Emirates. He was a previous Grand Mufti of Egypt.

Thankfully, the Grand Imam was a religious moderate. He was on record condemning the Islamic State of Iraq and Levant (ISIL), which over the previous four years had metastasized in Iraq and Syria, proclaiming a caliphate, reigning over cruelty and terror in all the lands they occupied.[62] ISIL had also established a network of connections with extremist affiliates in other countries, which carried out high-profile terrorist attacks abroad. ISIL propaganda was continuing to inspire a series of lone-wolf attacks in the West. The Grand Imam had already declared that ISIL exported a false Islam.

We met the Imam in a modesty-appointed room with a freakishly long table for large meetings. He sat at the head of the table in gray robes with a snow-white koofi kofi kufi topi cap. He was classic Egyptian handsome with dark, thoughtful eyes and a trimmed beard, more salt than pepper. He was generous with his time and our hour-long conversation covered a lot of ground.

We started easy and asked him whether Islam and democracy were compatible. "Yes and no," he replied. "No, if democracy produces ethical deviations, if individual freedom is used for destructive things against the nature of man. Yes, if democracy liberates humans, gives them high morale, and makes all people truly equal."

I raised terrorism, dealing with extremism, and the horroresque appeal of ISIL. I also asked him about his relationship with the Wahhabi School and whether he would issue a fatwa (legal opinion) to underscore acceptable behavior according to the Muslim faith. "99% of Muslims do not need another fatwa," he said calmly. (I remember thinking that 1% of extremist Muslims were proving highly destructive, so why not issue a fatwa to highlight their acts of injustice.) The Imam went on, "The Wahhabi School is only one school of thought and Islam reflects a broader view of life than their narrow vision."

On ISIL, he slowly shook his head and commented, "I condemn all attacks. A Muslim should only fight when defending himself. We must have tolerance, because all people are different, even our fingerprints are unique. No one group should control another with their views. One individual can't control the heart of another." He paused for a moment, then finished, "People cannot be unified under one religion. Our supreme responsibility is creating relationships with one another, knowing each other, respecting each other, being acquainted." We all nodded at these sensible words.

At the end of the session, I gifted the Imam a clock, telling him that his voice was probably the most important in the Middle East right now, and that his messages were vital. I wished him Godspeed in communicating the true meaning of his storied religion, finishing with "We are sure you will make the most of every minute as the Grand Imam."

To our surprise, we were then invited to see first-hand how the Grand Imam was attempting to counter extremism. We were guided upstairs to a 24/7 operations center called the "Al Azhar Observer." A dedicated team of 65 educated Muslims were engaged online, in blogs and chat rooms interacting with people around the world in eight different languages. They were all tapping on keyboards, countering extremist propaganda, clarifying Islamic tenets, undistorting warped interpretations of the Koran, Hadiths, and Sunnah. The Grand Imam was not just a single voice for moderation, he had assembled a chorus of voices for moderation, which was now continuously engaged on social media to blunt the tide of radicalism. A member of his team quietly confessed to us, "I just wish we had started this earlier."

Within a year of our visit, the Grand Imam proclaimed Salafis and Wahhabis were not Sunnis. He blasted Takfiri terrorism and even issued a fatwa calling Shia the fifth school of Islam in an attempt to bridge what had been a wrenching religious divide in Islam for centuries. He met Pope Francis twice and signed a "Document on Human Fraternity" in 2019.

The Grand Imam exerted halcyonic influence over time, tempering many Muslims who were tempted to provide financial, informational, or physical support to Islamic extremist groups. And yet, in the big picture, moderate voices arrived late in the Global War on Terror. For years, more concerted and powerful efforts could have been applied in countless countries, by many imams, to invest in a different climate regarding the nature of their religion, what constituted just action, and what behaviors were truly righteous. For too long, before and after the turn of the century, moderate

Muslims were meek or muted, giving oxygen to radicals, who were happy to fill vacuums with their dark narratives and bloody visions of global jihad.

These unresolved struggles within the Islamic community reminded that investing in one's climate entails regular gardening, and purposeful action to tend to one's environment. Leaders must cultivate their respective climates as a distinct, unceasing line of effort, something that goes beyond simply pursuing an organization's mission and vision. To this end, they must often be willing to invest in the blind, because immediate results may not be discernable. They must stay confident that their proactive work to build a solid culture will carry a long-term payoff. The primary metric that a climate has been made right with preventative shaping is when people are fired up for all the right reasons. Similarly, a key indicator of a broken climate is when leaders find themselves putting out fires for all the wrong reasons.

While the Grand Imam was a definitive force for good, the relatively weak efforts of moderate Muslims around the world for years, who failed to convincingly project a more balanced view of their religion in global discourse, showed the terrible consequences of benign neglect, of acting only until it was almost too late to make a difference. In the macrocosm, it showed the penalty of ceding one's climate to chance and fate, the traditional harbingers of misfortune.

➤ A senior leader's imperative is to set and shape the climate—the prevailing norms, mores, attitudes, perceptions, expectations, and ethical spirit of a place. This takes time and creativity, frequent cranks on the flywheel, plus an unending engagement of head and heart to nourish an environment that fosters dignity, respect, tolerance, transparency, trust, accountability, and other winning traits of successful teams.

➤ The real secret to a durable and thriving climate is getting it to reinforce itself organically by members who are committed to protecting and sustaining their collective values and culture.[63]

➤ It's better to spend time uplifting with proactive prevention rather than draining one's energy on reactive consequence management. Either do wellness well or be ill with illness.

➤ Everything is easier and more profitable when one's organizational atmosphere is right. Everything is harder and costlier when it's not. Invest in your climate and your climate will invest in you.

35

BRANDING

*"An idea can turn to magic or dust, depending
on the talent that rubs against it."*

– Bill Bernach[64]

Military leaders innately understand the power of symbols to inspire, cement a sense of belonging, and unite the troops. Egyptians used animal skin flags etched with their Gods as far back as 3000 BCE. The Greeks painted their round aspis and argive shields with blazons. Roman legions carried vexillum and signum banners to the far reaches of their empire. These trappings not only gave warriors their identity but served as rallying points for those asked to risk everything for a cause. Not much has changed over the millennia.

One of the first things I give attention to when in a leadership role is whether or not our organization's emblems are fit for function. Are we bearing the right standards that will marshal the spirits and generate pride in the distinctive contributions we offer?

My first command was a large information and communications technology unit called the Hopper Information Service Center. Anyone in the IT business knows morale is a constant issue. There's little winning in that line of work. You either break even because all systems are working as expected or you lose because something's broken. A paucity of external customer-oriented recognition puts a premium on developing internal sources of pride and recognition. Turns out we didn't even have a motto. Also, our longstanding command emblem was dark and uninspiring. Collaborating with my leadership team, we created a second command emblem that served as the reverse side of a coin. We intermixed all the sailor rating symbols such as a lightning bolt, quill, and magnifying glass, and added classic IT symbols like gears, circular arrows, and even a cloud, all displayed in bright primary colors. Our motto became "Proudly Delivering IT for Intelligence." That put some sizzle in our steak.

We also thought people should connect better with their namesake. We had a few pictures of Admiral Grace Hopper on display, older ones of her frail and wizened. We replaced some of those with Grace in her prime working during the 1940s and 1950s on the world's first computers. We also created a history and heritage display on our main corridor featuring her background and pivotal role in bringing the Navy into the modern age. A TV recording of her funny interview with David Letterman in the 1980s played on a loop, so everyone could hear Grace's voice and laughter whenever they passed by in the corridor. These steps brought our forebear alive and more relatable to hundreds of our junior sailors and civilians. Efforts like this, along with others, helped recharge command spirits and we saw a tangible improvement in the level of unit confidence, self-esteem, and pride.

Five years later, I was the third commanding officer of the Joint Intelligence Operations Center at U.S. Cyber Command and inherited neither a unit emblem nor a motto. Essentially, we were in a tough business and standard-less. So, once again, we lifted a new banner. Our logomark became Lady Liberty's hand holding the torch, golden rays of tiny 1s and 0s emanating from the flame. Below the command title on the curved seal, we added the tagline, "Lighting the Way in Cyberspace." The phrase resonated with our personnel, the best gauge being the number of emblazoned coffee mugs sold. Sometimes leaders need to enliven their history and heritage, sometimes they need to birth it.

Branding is worth one's attention, it's not a nice-to-have. Leaders must devote quality time to getting their compositions and designs right. They should understand how the anatomy of different symbols and vocabulary can dial up the power settings of team pride and performance. Carefully capturing the essence of their organization's identity and highlighting true incarnations of its purpose through specialized language and imagery can simultaneously ground and lift people to new heights.

> A leader's skill at branding and marketing has the power to either accelerate or decelerate any endeavor. Leaders must use all tools at their disposal to win support, build momentum, and keep positive inertia going.

> One's symbols should be distinctive, simple, succinct, hip, and thematically consonant with mission and purpose. Done creatively and well, brands provide instant recognition. They fire the mind. They possess staying power. They become a source of pride. They entice people to partake.[65]

> A brand distills something to its essence. It captures a kernel of meaningfulness, a compelling pith, the soul of a thing simultaneously reflecting both its personality and character. A well-crafted one rings true and resonates in ways that will emotionally attract, connect, and inspire people.[66]

36

MOTIVATION

"It is not the mountain we conquer but ourselves."

– Sir Edmund Hillary

I disseminated a number of my leadership "minutes" through-out the J2 intelligence staff and Joint Intelligence Operations Center (JIOC) during my time in the Pacific in Hawaii. I never really knew what specific impact they had on the workforce, even though a few individuals would always take time to send me back kind notes of appreciation. Then one day a request came through the suggestion box to write a leadership "minute" on how to stay motivated.

I had a feeling that the person who submitted the suggestion was a particular senior analyst, one of our top performers. I had worked with him over twenty years earlier in the same intelligence facility on Oahu and highly respected his intellect. He had worked for ten 4-star Combatant Commanders and at least 15 Directors of Intelligence in his career. He was bright, hard-working, experienced, and supremely dedicated. His network of expert contacts in the theater, in academia, think tanks, and the rest of the Intelligence Community was without compare. Not only could he quickly find answers to complicated questions, but he could also whip out a Shakespearean-quality product in short order. He was a national treasure. I would privately call him up on our classified televideo line to consult him on the toughest problems I faced as the two-star intelligence director.

Yet now I was deeply concerned he was burned out and considering an exit strategy. I understood why. The rise of China and its intensifying activities across the Western Pacific were creating more work than ever before. Despite senior officials talking for years about pivoting and rebalancing to the Pacific, it didn't translate into enough new blood in the intelligence center. The busiest people remained overloaded, overtaxed, and overstressed. It was no wonder the senior analyst, who I saw as the equivalent of our atlas vertebra in the intelligence center, was ready to call it quits.

Most of the time leaders do things with the whole team in mind, but sometimes they have to do something with one team member in mind. I wrote the "minute" specifically for the senior analyst, though it was disguised as another group think piece. I wanted to recognize the toll on his life, the sacrifices he'd made, the relentlessness he'd endured. I also wanted to let him know that it would be OK to leave the job if he concluded it was just misery, if he couldn't find enough room for satisfaction or happiness in the mix. I had to offer him the option to leave and reassure him he had freedom of choice in the matter. And this had to come from me, the J2, the one that needed him the most. Still, I hoped that my prescriptive advice on sharing burdens, taking a break, and taking some time for himself might ease his burden if he partook.

The next day, the senior analyst and I were reviewing an assessment on the televideo net and he wrapped up with an understated, "Hey, by the way, nice leadership minute." "Think so?" I said, looking carefully at him. He just smiled, knowingly. I smiled back. I ended the call, breathing a sigh of relief.

It is easy in difficult or tedious assignments to lose steam. It's just a matter of time. Motivations fade no matter how capable you might be. It's the black gift of drudgery when life seems to solely revolve around a single wretched axis. These are the times when leadership matters the most. Leaders may or may not be able to alter the circumstances that produce hard times and anguish, but they must rise when it counts to serve as the beacon of light that sustains hope, buoys the spirit, and sees things through.

> Everyone will feel a sense of decayed inspiration at some point, perhaps from a combination of accumulated wear and tear, high workload, persistent stress, or simply changing life priorities. In those cases, it's essential to take breaks. To breathe. To think. To rest. To let others stand in.

> It can be helpful to journey back to your origin story, re-inspect the pilings and footings, revisit the profoundly important reason you started, and try to recapture the fountainhead of passion that led you to pursue a certain line of work in the first place.

> Never underestimate the amazing powers of rejuvenation offered by simply eating, sleeping, exercising, and socializing with people you like and love.

> Leaders must also do their part to set a sustainable pace or risk losing valuable people. Not caring is the quickest way to lose your best people.

37

MICROMANAGEMENT?

"Build for your team a feeling of oneness,
of dependence on one another and of
strength to be derived by unity."

– Vince Lombardi

In my last job in the Navy as the Commander of the Office of Naval Intelligence, I once again encountered a disturbing misconception among some juniors that seniors should mind their own business and just let experts do their jobs. While it is true that corporate leadership is a full-time job and smart delegation is vital for any sizable unit, excessive under-involvement and failure to mind details at the middle to upper levels can unintentionally run an organization into shoal water.

ONI was already in dangerous shallows and had struck a few rocks. In my first town hall, I broke the news to the workforce saying, "ONI's ship is listing," an allusion to a vessel taking on water and tilting to one side. I shared that ONI analysts were unquestioned world-class experts on foreign maritime forces, especially their technical capabilities and developmental trends. It was true many customers of ONI expertise raved over the support they were receiving. Certain elements of ONI were performing brilliantly, led by experienced civilians and military leaders. Those people had earned a long leash and required minimal oversight.

But ONI was falling short on some basic ingredients for success in a modern intelligence agency. For example, we needed to reimagine our product line. One of the most significant holes in our swing was that we had no executive product. To that end, shortly after I arrived in command, we started a new all-source flagship line named Waypoints facilitated by an Executive Product Improvement Cell (EPIC). Waypoints were short two-page reports with graphics designed to rapidly and succinctly cover a major maritime topic, adding opportunity analysis. Opportunity analysis had largely been missing from ONI products, although it was a well-known intelligence tradecraft technique that offered ideas on what operational forces and decision-makers could potentially consider doing with the intelligence.

Articulating anything complex with clarity, deep insight, and pith is taxing. Brevity isn't easy. Many ONI analysts had been caught in the Mark Twain trap: "I didn't have time to write you a short letter, so I wrote you a long one." Also, many analysts remained specialists in narrow fields of study, highly stove-piped, deep not broad. Few integrators existed to connect all the dots, and provide cross-cutting analysis with sweep and relevance. Further, an inordinate number of junior analysts had yet to accumulate life experiences embedded with their customers, and many mid-level supervisors' experiences were dated or decayed.

One of our most serious challenges in creating this new premier product line was restoring symbiotic connections with customers, especially those in overseas theaters, which had frayed during the COVID-19 pandemic. You can't write analysis in the blind. You must be in circles of trust. You need context. You must know what your customers already know, what they need to know, their top concerns, the problems they are trying to solve, and where you can add genuine value. You must keep ken on what policies policymakers are considering, what operations operational forces are executing, what plans planners are refining, and what force designers are designing into future forces. We began resurging people out of our headquarters, encouraging and rewarding them for super-connecting with partners.

For all these aforementioned reasons, in the beginning, ONI struggled to get Waypoints off the ground at the world-class level required to support principals in the national security community. I found myself involved in shaping the topic selection, structure, and content of our executive works. Analysts, supervisors, and leadership teams were routinely invited into my corner office to pull apart a topic, review assumptions, and dissect draft assessments. I served as an extra third-level reviewer to ensure the writing and analysis were truly ready for dissemination, seeing it through an executive's eyes, contributing insights from 33 years of experience, much of it right next to senior leaders in important positions in the Navy, Pentagon, and Combatant Commands.

I also held uniformed, Fleet-experienced officers in top leadership positions accountable for what their teams were producing. I expected them to apply their hard-won skills, regional expertise, and knowledge of the missions and customers they worked with in previous assignments to improve our intelligence output.

These dynamics gave rise to a feeling in junior and mid-level ranks of micromanagement. Why were the two-star admiral, senior executives, and captains personally spending time reviewing and editing? Weren't they supposed to trust downward after setting the vision, objectives, goals, and performance milestones? You know, put things in motion and then get out of the way? Not for the first time, I recognized how misused the term "micromanagement" had become in modern-day parlance, and how the mid and senior-level leaders' fear of being labeled one had shaped much of our enterprise into a dangerous laissez-faire culture.

For the record, leaders up and down any chain of command must be involved in the matters for which they are responsible. That frequently requires specific knowledge and familiarity with details. How deeply and how often they are involved swings in proportion to the degree of difficulty, novelty, and/or priority of a task. The appetite for critical minutiae typically will grow commensurate with the strategic import, external visibility, or stakes of a project. One of the most important responsibilities of a leader is to know when they must apply their personal attention to a problem because there are some things only they can do. Put another way, when a senior leader remains aloof and disengaged, subordinate team members can struggle unnecessarily longer and more tortuously through a problem. The latter approach is a form of irresponsible non-teaming.

Delegating works when the talent base is fully qualified to meet a challenge. When it's not, then the whole team, top to bottom, must come together to make something work. At times, particularly when kick-starting a new venture, all expertise within the lifelines may need to be channeled until the job is done right. Then and only then should a team consider transitioning to a more delegable rhythm, a mainstreaming mode, where it might be possible to flip on the autopilot switch.

Like all superb executive intelligence, the creation of each ONI Waypoint report ultimately took extraordinary teamwork, integration of insights at all levels, and many people sweating details. The accolades rolled in after each product was delivered. Fleet and Joint Force Commanders, top policymakers, interagency principals, and many others shared their praise and deep appreciation. Our executive intelligence was not just being read, but eagerly consumed, and it was shaping major decisions in time to make a difference.

Micromanagement is not when a leader is seemingly too involved with the team in pursuit of a mission. A micromanager is someone who makes the team all about the leader instead of the mission. Knowing the difference is key to fostering a culture that values the power of both vertical and horizontal collaboration to generate holistic team success.

> Many developing leaders have become dangerously gun-shy about immersing themselves in team projects and many subordinates have falsely come to believe that any boss worth their salt should keep their distance.

> A micromanager is someone who never trusts their people, who keeps employees in the dark, who is disinterested in others' opinions, who stymies innovation, and who puts his/her ego ahead of everything else. The main weakness of a micromanager is not over-involvement, but a failure to lead in genuine partnerships with others.

> Exceptional leaders build trust through active involvement, deliver context and clarity for employees, and collaborate for collective success. They aren't just cheerleaders and they don't just float in clouds watching from on high.

> Leaders who have both "down and in" and "up and out" responsibilities understand that carrying out their role requires them to know relevant micro-knowledge. These leaders can't and shouldn't try to be experts at everything, but they need sufficient information and insight to remain credible, and to do their jobs right.

TRANSFORMING YOUR WORLD

LIFTING GREAT WEIGHTS

Premium-grade links and smoothly interlocked chains contribute exceptional bearing strength for their ultimate lift tests. However, gearing up for the heaviest of loads, either to relieve pressures that hold one down or take endeavors to new heights, takes extra dexterity. Heavy-duty lifting work requires rigging with the right tackle, hooking up implements ranging from master rings, shackles, and multi-leg chains that must be ready to undergo extreme hoisting pressures. Taking tension requires an exquisite understanding of fulcrum and tipping points, maintaining proper angles of lift, and careful balancing throughout an entire operation. Chapters in this final section address leadership points that help power real change in one's professional field, bringing all the lifting techniques together to take things next level and achieve noteworthy outcomes.

38

PLAY TO STRENGTHS

*"Hide not your talents, they for use were
made. What's a sundial in the shade?"*

– Benjamin Franklin

Like a philharmonic conductor, Rear Admiral Sumner "Shap" Shapiro was a genius at maneuvering top talent into high-impact posts to achieve symphonic effects. In doing so, he helped win the Cold War. A veteran of the Korean War, former briefer to Chief of Naval Operations Arleigh Burke, and Assistant Naval Attache in Moscow, Shap served as the Director of Naval Intelligence during four critical years between 1978 and 1982. Those years would see well-placed intelligence professionals pierce the secrets of the Soviets, reevaluate Moscow's strategic calculus, persuade the Navy to overhaul its Maritime Strategy, and ultimately convince the Soviets they couldn't win a military conflict with the West.[67]

Shap assembled the finest naval intelligence professionals in the business to the Pentagon to work cheek by jowl with senior Navy warfare officers during this transformative time. Building on the talent-spotting brilliance of his predecessor, Rear Admiral Bobby Inman, he moved his top civilian analyst, Rich Haver, over from the Office of Naval Intelligence to focus on Soviet strategy. He approved Captain Bill Studeman to become executive assistant to the Vice Chief of Naval Operations. After Bill was promoted to one-star admiral,

Shap created a novel Navy staff position for him focused exclusively on perception management and deception to continue to capitalize on his grasp of strategic matters and innate cleverness.[68] Shap also positioned sharp, innovative thinkers like Captain Tom Brooks and Captain Bill Manthorpe close to him as his own executive assistants and special advisors.

These handpicked leaders, along with a few other bright up-and-coming mid-level intelligence officers, were in the vanguard of sweeping changes to the U.S. Navy, its doctrine, structure, equipment, and operational focus. They supported and helped lead the Advanced Technology Panel (ATP), which was established on the Navy staff in 1975 to advise the Chief of Naval Operations on sensitive intelligence and its implications.[69]

Collaboration that started in the 1960s between the Navy and the National Security Agency (NSA) to develop special techniques to penetrate Soviet designs had begun to yield fruit. By the mid-to late 1970s, those extraordinary investments in collection revealed startling new insights into how the Soviets thought, what they feared, and how they intended to use their military. These realizations, which were significantly different than previous assessments, required a complete rewrite of the Navy's strategy and how it should be leveraged to give America an unequivocal strategic advantage in the Cold War.[70]

For decades, the longstanding conception had been that if there was a major war in Europe, the Soviets would employ their Navy much like the Germans in World War II. They would project power into the Atlantic to cut off sea lines of communication that could enable the resupply of America's NATO allies. It was conventional wisdom that the Soviets had built a blue water Navy and invested in extensive capabilities in surface, subsurface, and air warfare to contest adversaries in fleet actions on the high seas. It was presumed adversary maritime "red forces" would engage in classic sea denial operations to isolate Europe and thus allow its superior numbers of conventional ground forces to roll over the continent to victory in any World War III scenario. The U.S. Navy had oriented its force structure, plans, and operational assumptions around this rational Mahanian judgment. However, the intelligence gathered and evaluated over time revealed a different truth altogether.

The reality was that the Soviets intended to use their Navy in a largely defensive strategy to protect their homeland against attacks from the sea and to guard their nuclear ballistic missile submarines (SSBNs) in bastions along their immediate flanks. Conventional general-purpose naval forces were to be employed primarily for layered barrier defenses. Soviet leaders did not want to risk momentous clashes between battle group concentrations far from home waters, because they believed naval battles would not be decisive in war. Instead, they believed maintaining fleets-in-being, especially a survivable SSBN force, would allow them to control conflict escalation, keep U.S. forces at bay, deter nuclear strikes, and retain a valuable strategic card when negotiating war termination terms.

Many U.S. admirals found these new insights on Soviet thinking almost unbelievable because they were so utterly counter-intuitive to the naval mind.[71] They needed convincing, so Shap sent his most colorful narrator into the fray. Rich Haver became the "St. Paul of the movement, going forth among Gentiles (unrestricted line officers) and preaching the Gospel. The conversion rate was astounding."[72] He warned about mirror-imaging, explained the depth of Army influence on Soviet thinking, and laid out the differences in their perceptions and mindset.

Shap then used his elite team of senior officers to help the admiralty figure out how to exploit the intelligence and convert it into U.S. naval capabilities, operations, and actions that would attack Soviet plans and alter their strategic calculus.[73] This approach eventually bred a revised Maritime Strategy, one that emphasized offensive naval capabilities and demonstrations along the strategic approaches to the USSR, which would reinforce Soviet fears and continue to bias them toward prioritizing their defenses.[74]

A key element of the U.S. Navy's approach was to persistently show the vulnerability of Soviet SSBNs to U.S. anti-submarine forces.[75]

If the Soviet leaders couldn't gain enough confidence in their surviv-ability, Moscow's willingness to resort to conflict in Europe could be reduced by a great measure. Throughout the 1980s, the U.S. Navy's success in pursuing this strategy eroded the confidence of leaders in Moscow and ultimately contributed to the sense of strategic fatal-ism that set conditions for the collapse of the USSR by the end of the decade.[76]

President Reagan marveled at the brilliance of both the Navy and the Intelligence Community for their contributions during this period. In 1981, Haver briefed the President, Secretary of State Shultz, and a few other top advisors in the White House on what was being learned about the Soviets and how we were learning it. Realizing the dangers Navy forces were undertaking to acquire criti-cal intelligence, Reagan interjected "Where do you find such patri-ots?" Haver replied, "They're just average Americans doing extraordi-nary things, Mr. President." At the end of the meeting, Reagan shook Haver's hand and then observed, "You know, you're a good story-teller. That's the key to leadership. People have to believe your story, then they'll believe you."

A few weeks later, Haver was called back to the Oval Office for an impromptu meeting with the President. Reagan handed Haver a glossy picture of the White House. On it, the President had penned a thank you note to the special team at NSA that had helped acquire the earth-shaking intelligence: "From a grateful nation that does not know what you've done, and from an infinitely more grateful President who does." The President also gifted a cigar box to accom-pany the photo. "I bought that myself," he said smiling. "I made the Secret Service escort me across Lafayette Square last night to buy the cigars in person." He paused. "Let me correct that. I borrowed money from Nancy ... I don't have any." Haver cautioned, "I hope you'll pay her back." "Probably not!" chuckled Reagan.

Haver drove up that evening to Ft. Meade and presented the President's tokens to the responsible NSA Section Chief, who imme-diately started to tear up. The Chief gathered all his people around, showed them the White House tributes, and then exclaimed "That's why we work! That's why we do what we do!" The office erupted in cheers and clapping.[77]

Leaders plant the seeds of success when they play to people's strengths. Admiral Shapiro not only knew the deck of talent at his disposal, he positioned them where their natural skills would thrive. His careful placement of Naval Intelligence luminaries contributed to a historic decision by a reluctant Navy to pivot in a different direction, at great expense and effort. Those epic adjustments hinged on the throw weight of just a select few, whose aptitudes, expertise, and savvy were deployed at the right place at the right time to help change the course of history. At the end of the day, consequential talent management is simply about putting square pegs in square holes.

> Awakening the potential of those around you is one of your greatest charges as a leader.[78] Focus on what they do best and nourish it for all it's worth.[79]

> While leaders must help people overcome shortcomings that are vital to the skillsets required at work, deploying people where they naturally excel will allow them to gain confidence, achieve success faster, and set them on a virtuous cycle toward greatness.

> Equally important is how you mix people and their respective capabilities against certain projects. Particular combinations can create even more powerful effects. This is the art of leadership in its most basic form.

39

RESULTS

"Pursue one great decisive aim with force and determination."

– Carl von Clausewitz

I only spent one year as the commander of the U.S. Cyber Command Joint Intelligence Operations Center (CYBERCOM JIOC) before I was selected for admiral in 2016, but it was an impactful time. We faced a spectrum of cyber challenges from our command headquarters in Ft. Meade, Maryland, where we were collocated with the National Security Agency (NSA). It felt strange yet somehow fitting to walk the same hallways as my father when he was Director of the NSA twenty years earlier. Time for my own rite of passage as an intelligence professional in the heart of the Puzzle Palace.

At that time, and still today, major state-sponsored cyber threats were daggers at the heart of America's vital organs. Russia had been interfering during U.S. elections and continued to rampantly insert divisive content across American social media spaces to amplify political polarization in our country. The Russian gambit was to dilute U.S. focus on Russia by sowing so much divisiveness inside our nation that our leadership would be preoccupied with internal matters rather than spending time executing an active foreign policy.

Russian troll farms crafted sensationalized feeds, which they posted using fake personas, to roil emotions and keep hate on the agenda for average Americans. Russia saw repeated successes in manipulating American citizens to see one another as their greatest enemy. It was a cheap way for Moscow to weaken our democracy and accelerate what Putin hoped would be America's declining influence in the world.

Both Russia and China had also worked for years to penetrate our nation's critical infrastructure, which included our energy sector, water systems, information technology domain, communications architecture, transportation networks, and defense industrial base. Moscow and Beijing were mapping our vulnerabilities and laying the groundwork for cyberattacks that could paralyze our society in times of crisis. Russia and China were spending substantial energy developing trump cards that would enable them to achieve strategic effects on our homeland. Russia and China were not cooperating, as far as we knew, but they were both pursuing non-nuclear escalation options to have at the ready in a pinch.[80]

China was particularly dangerous because it brought scale to bear in cyberspace. Thousands of Chinese hackers that belonged to the People's Liberation Army (PLA) Strategic Support Forces toiled each day to penetrate American society. The Chinese government also employed mercenary Chinese hackers from private companies. China had been engaged in widespread digital spying and cyber-enabled espionage for many years, exploiting accesses to steal intellectual property from U.S. companies.[81] Total theft was estimated to be $250 billion to $600 billion each year, cumulatively trillions of dollars of innovative U.S. technology over the years.[82] Pillaged trade secrets, research and development knowledge, and cutting-edge technology were all funneled to Chinese companies and their military to supercharge their rapid rise. A former director of the NSA, General Keith Alexander, called this effort "the greatest transfer of wealth in human history."[83]

China's industrial and technological exploitation continues unabated today, helping China to build immense comprehensive national strength, resulting in a remarkably changed balance of power between the world's top two superpowers. In the main,

Americans continue to underestimate and underappreciate the degree to which this cyber hemorrhaging is jeopardizing the nation's long-term economic and security interests.

Even while tracking these nation-state threats and supporting coordinated efforts to counter them, we were charged to support operations in the Middle East against the Islamic State of Iraq and the Levant (ISIL), or Daesh. In late 2014, President Obama directed the Defense Department to degrade and ultimately destroy ISIL, which was responsible for horrific atrocities, including public mass executions in Syria and Iraq. What emerged was Operation Inherent Resolve, which used a combination of U.S. Special Operations advisory support to proxy forces on the ground, intelligence, and air strikes to support partner forces.

In 2016, as Abu Bakr al-Baghdadi's ISIL was slowly and steadily being rolled back, Admiral Mike Rogers, commander of U.S. Cyber Command, established a dedicated Joint Task Force-Ares (JTF-Ares) to help further weaken ISIL's global online presence and appeal. Much of ISIL's financial support, recruitment successes, and malign influence had been enabled by the Caliphate's highly active media arm.

JTF-Ares moved out, connected with like-minded international partners, and began conducting network exploitation and offensive cyber operations to disrupt ISIL propagandists. As the Joint Intelligence Operations Center commander, I lent substantial intelligence support to JTF-Ares to go after this abhorrent foreign terrorist organization while balancing our other nation-state priorities. Ultimately, four of my eight divisions (collections, analysis, targeting, and human intelligence operations), representing a big chunk of my 300-member command, provided direct intelligence aid to the JTF.[84]

Throughout 2016 and 2017, these concentrated anti-ISIL efforts delivered both physical and virtual blows to ISIL, eventually bringing it to its knees. Clever cyber operations destroyed ISIL media infrastructure, redirected supporters, manipulated their banner online products, cut off financial flows, sowed distrust between ISIL members, and enabled kinetic targeting of ISIL media leaders. Before I left Ft. Meade, ISIL's capital of Raqqa in Syria and the population center they had captured in Mosul in Iraq had fallen. Their bloody rule over wide tracts of the Mesopotamian region was nearing its end.[85]

My time as U.S. Cyber Command reminded me of the importance of orienting one's energy around getting results, and doing one's utmost to achieve real outcomes. That almost always requires painful resource calls and elevating measures of effectiveness over measures of performance when judging progress. It also demands discernment in knowing what to put first, and when.

> Never muddle hard work and success. Don't confuse motion with action, heat for light. Give your top priorities the billing they deserve. Keep first things first.

> The truest measures of success are how well the organization's mission has been advanced, whether a vision is more manifest, and how much difference has been made in the real world.

> An execution-oriented organization is obsessed with achieving real progress—better quality service, greater responsiveness, expeditious delivery, improved products, quicker decision-making, enhanced partner trust, strengthened loyalty, influence, value, profit, advantage, victory.

40

DECISIVENESS

"Misplaced caution, more ruinous than the most daring venture."

– Alfred Thayer Mahan

I bore witness to a fine example of swiftness and sound, decisive judgment in action in the spring of 2009. At the time, I was a commander and the senior intelligence officer (also known as "N2" or "deuce") for Carrier Strike Group Eight deployed aboard the USS *Eisenhower* (CVN-69). The aircraft carrier and our cruiser escort were operating in the Northern Arabian Sea east of Oman, launching aircraft up a corridor leading through Pakistan to Afghanistan. Newly inaugurated President Obama had announced a new strategy for Afghanistan, adding more troops to assist the Afghan Army and Police, and focusing on countering a resurgent Taliban and foreign fighters flooding into southern Afghanistan. Our aircraft provided surveillance, jamming against improvised explosive devices, and close air support for any "troops in contact," a military term for deadly firefights on the ground.

A traditional Carrier Strike Group at the time was composed of a carrier, cruiser, and 1–3 destroyers and/or frigates. Because we faced no major naval threats on the seas, the Fifth Fleet Commander and three-star vice admiral in charge of Naval Forces Central Command would routinely disaggregate, or disperse, ships to deal with other Middle East challenges beyond the war in Afghanistan.

Those included operating in the Arabian Gulf to protect U.S. and partner interests from malign behavior from Iran, intercepting narcotics shipments from South Asia and the Makran Coast that provided revenue for the Taliban, supporting counterterrorism operations against Al Qaeda fighters in Yemen and affiliates like Al Shabaab in Somalia, and helping patrol the Gulf of Aden with other friendly navies in a multinational effort to stem a growing tide of piracy off the Horn of Africa.

A couple of our Strike Group ships, USS *Bainbridge* (DDG-96) and USS *Halyburton* (FFG-40), were operating near the Gulf of Aden when Somali pirates boarded the U.S. container ship *Maersk Alabama* as it was making for Kenya about 250 miles off the Somali Coast.[86] It was the first time in almost 200 years that pirates were able to hijack an American-flagged ship. The pirates ultimately failed to fully capture the ship thanks to the bravery of the crew, and the pirates decided instead to take Captain Richard Phillips hostage and escape on the ship's 5-ton lifeboat. The pirates intended to make for shore and ransom the captain.

Rescue operations were immediately put in motion. Our destroyer and frigate arrived on the scene in time to herd the lifeboat away from land until the lifeboat ran out of fuel. If the pirates had made it to shore, the chances of saving Captain Phillips would have been exponentially harder. After long hours of rolling in rough seas without making any headway, the pirates finally agreed to be taken in tow by the USS *Bainbridge* while negotiations took place over Captain Phillips.

The hostage situation had been monitored and reported to the President, who authorized a number of actions as the crisis unfolded. Within 24 hours of the decision to deploy Navy Special Warfare, scores of SEALs and support personnel arrived on the scene and distributed themselves between a command element established aboard USS *Boxer* (LHD-4), an amphibious ship that had also maneuvered into the general area, and a tactical element on the USS *Bainbridge*. Rules of engagement were rapidly clarified, with the SEALs operating as the main element and all other naval forces acting as supporting elements. If Captain Phillip's life was threatened, the on-scene SEAL commander was authorized to take action as required to save him.

Snipers took firing positions and the lifeboat tow line was shortened over time. At one point, a pirate pointed his AK-47 into the back of Captain Phillips in a life-threatening gesture. The decision to act was quickly made on-scene, but only if the snipers could simultaneously take out all three pirates, who were positioned in different locations inside the lifeboat. The SEALs calmly waited until the exact moment when they had three clean shots and fired in quick succession, killing the pirates and bringing the multi-day crisis to an end.

This operation proved to be a unique test of rapidly meshing conventional and unconventional forces at sea to resolve a time-sensitive maritime hostage rescue situation.[87] Not everything went smoothly or perfectly. For example, sharing near real-time video feeds from available manned and unmanned intelligence, surveillance, and reconnaissance assets was troublesome throughout. Yet the series of smart and forthright actions by multiple decision-makers at various levels made all the difference and ultimately saved Captain Phillips.

Whatever challenges a leader faces, it is worth remembering that people are counting on them to move out thoughtfully and purposely. One doesn't need to be a SEAL to be confident and resolute. Successful leaders in every career field routinely demonstrate a bias for action and good judgment regarding how to handle crises. Doubt and uncertainty will always disconcert in a predicament, but leaders must not allow themselves to be paralyzed by indecision, otherwise, their ship will be left to yaw rudderless in roughening seas.

> Decisiveness does not necessarily equate to instantaneous judgments, but it is about making good calls in time to make a difference. Beware paralysis by doubt.

> You must initiate action even while the picture remains hazy and incomplete. Take charge or someone else will take the helm.[88]

> Decisiveness is neither rashness nor a rush to judgment, it's about the skill and confidence to make well-timed, resolute decisions to march forward even in fog. It's the place where knowledge and instinct intersect.

41

TEAMING

"We cannot live unto ourselves and remain strong."

– George C. Marshall

As the Director for Intelligence at the Indo-Pacific Command, I had a front-row seat to one of the most significant geopolitical shifts in the 21ˢᵗ century, India's reorientation away from China and toward closer relations with the U.S. and other Western democratic nations. Capitalizing on this strategic opportunity involved reaching out to unfamiliar players, breaking new bureaucratic ground, and patiently learning what combinations of actions would evolve the partnership at a pace acceptable to both parties. Intensified U.S.-India cooperation became a test of bilateral teaming under a bright international spotlight.

In an amazing display of geopolitical autism, Beijing allowed an aggressive PLA Western Military Region commander to unilaterally push into multiple contested areas with India along the Line of Actual Control in the Ladakh region in 2020. The Ladakh area in India's union territory of eastern Jammu and Kashmir is a cold, barren mountainous section of the Himalayas rising 10,000–25,000 feet above sea level. A Sino-Indian War had been fought in the area in 1962.

China's deployment of troops, heavy equipment, and encampments into Indian territory and adjacent buffer zones immediately set off a crisis. China claimed India was at fault because India had been improving road and bridge infrastructure in Indian territory along the approaches to the border. Hypocritically, China had been doing the same for years on their side of the disputed territory, but on an even greater scale.

A series of skirmishes between forward troops escalated in June 2020 to a bloody melee, resulting in the deaths of 20 Indian soldiers and as many as 35 Chinese soldiers.[89] Adhering to a long-standing agreement to avoid using firearms along the border, the fight in Galwan Valley in the Karakoram mountains became a six-hour, nighttime brawl involving stones, spears, machetes, iron bars, spiked clubs, and rods wrapped in barbed wire. Some soldiers died after being pushed off ridges to their deaths or were swept away in the sub-zero, fast-moving river nearby. Additional clashes and tactical encounters occurred along the border over months, and both sides reinforced their approach zones with thousands more soldiers, artillery, tanks, missile systems, and aircraft before a series of Corps Commander talks stabilized the situation by early 2021.

In the end, between 2020 and 2023, an estimated 2,000 square kilometers of Indian land was ceded to China through a series of equidistant withdrawal agreements, which lopsidedly favored the aggressor. India ultimately lost access to 26 out of 65 patrolling points in Eastern Ladakh.[90] Whatever tactical gains China seemed to have achieved in this parched wasteland, however, failed to outweigh the ensuing strategic costs.

Due to the border clashes, Indians came to see China as a wolf in sheep's clothing—a manifested continental foe on its northeast flank today and possibly a maritime enemy on is southern flank tomorrow. India began to see the true colors of China's so-called "rise," a country with a creeping expansionist agenda in South Asia that mirrored China's heavy-handed influence efforts and coercion along other parts of China's periphery such as Nepal, Bhutan, Mekong, South China Sea, Taiwan, and the Senkakus.

India subsequently boycotted Chinese goods, banned apps, canceled infrastructure projects, and began to turn to friendlier nations to re-imagine India's economic, diplomatic, and security future. Of course, India remained fiercely independent and non-aligned, but these conditions created new openings for strengthened U.S.-India relations. The Indo-Pacific Command was one of the key entities involved in stepping across new thresholds to advance this partnership, and our intelligence apparatus was placed on point to help support New Delhi.

In the immediate aftermath of China's border incursions, and with approval from the White House, Secretary of Defense, and Director of National Intelligence, experts from our Joint Intelligence Operations Center Pacific (JIOCPAC) helped provide situational awareness to India on China's military movements. We used a variety of sources to provide clarity on the People's Liberation Army (PLA) force sizes, disposition, and activities. We looked deep into China, assessing force changes, evaluating intentions, delivering indications and warnings, and providing insights that India was able to use for its defensive planning and operations. The intelligence flows from the U.S. were unprecedented in volume, timeliness, and specificity. These prompt relays in crisis conditions probably did more to effect a strategic turn to the U.S. than any other one thing.[91]

I traveled long hours to New Delhi twice during my tour as the Director of Intelligence (J2), both times during the height of the COVID pandemic. Each time, city smog and smoke from stubble crop fires from the Indo-Gangetic plain hung over the capital creating an eerie dystopic glow. The atmosphere contributed to my sense of being a stranger in a strange land.

Most of my meetings took place in India's Secretariat Building that housed the Prime Minister's Office, Ministry of Defence, and Ministry of External Affairs. Known as South Block, the four-level building was domed in the center, walled in red and cream sandstone, enclosing large courtyards lined with wide open-air corridors. Strangely enough, hundreds of rhesus macaque monkeys roamed ledges around the building. The monkeys owned the building on weekends and weekday evenings. Our escorts told stories of territorial monkey troops occasionally chasing bureaucrats who worked late down the long corridors.

I was an odd specimen, an American admiral in my summer white uniform being escorted through the heart of India's government offices. Braving classic Indian heat and avoiding eye contact with passing macaques, I met with various senior Navy, defense, and intelligence officials. I was there to build trust, establish a basis for our new regional partnership, and discuss opportunities for a range of new intelligence agreements.

At India's Naval Intelligence headquarters, joined by U.S. Pacific Fleet representatives led by a gifted captain named Tony Butera, we hammered out language for a Maritime Information Sharing Technical Agreement (MISTA). On a second trip to India almost a year later, just hours before a U.S.-India Ministerial 2+2 meeting between Defense and Foreign Ministers, I signed the MISTA in an official ceremony with the Indian Navy.[92] This signing set the stage for follow-on intelligence agreements with the Army and Air Force. Inking these accords, along with other efforts such as the formation of the Quadrilateral Security Dialogue (aka Quad) between India, the U.S., Australia, and Japan, signaled a sea change in strategic cooperation in the Indo-Pacific. All are largely thanks to Beijing's continuing series of strategic miscalculations and threatening actions in the region.

My India experiences reminded me that becoming a trusted partner takes an inordinate amount of time and effort. It requires a mindset of coming together as equals. At the international level, it becomes vital to know the culture, history, sociology, and associated sensitivities of a foreign counterpart, and, most importantly, to convert that understanding into an ability to exercise strategic patience.

Years ago, I heard a scholar describe Americans as "generous cowboys with short attention spans." True teaming, whether strengthening existing partnerships or forging new ones, requires shedding this native hastiness for an equanimity that leads to more respectful, meaningful, and richer relationships with others. Long and abiding attention spans will prove more essential than ever in a century marked by intensified global strategic competition between major powers, which will necessitate finding mutually beneficial concord with all nations no matter their size. These dynamics will present a true team of teams test for American leaders.

> Complex endeavors with multiple stakeholders in high-tempo, high-stakes environments demand tighter teaming than ever before.[93] Building bridges expands one's sensor system, deepens understanding, enlarges context, increases fidelity, fosters trust, and supercharges performance.

> Strengthening muscles across boundary lines involves repeatedly exercising human connections, sharing time and resources, and staying true to commitments.

> Becoming a reliable partner means doing what you say you will do, which leads to credibility and influence. The opposite is true—if you fail to deliver on promises, the ensuing reputational damage can be difficult to recover.

> Sparking and stoking collaboration across the wide expanses enables leaders to haul their most substantial burdens to their most providential heights.

42

PATIENCE

"The two most powerful warriors are patience and time."

– Leo Tolstoy

I had to bolt on an extra reserve tank of patience to my system for the challenges I faced as the Director for Intelligence (J2) at U.S. Southern Command (SOUTHCOM) in Miami. I learned we were never going to quickly resolve any of the assorted security challenges affecting the Caribbean, Central America, and South America. As the Combatant Command with the least resources at our disposal, SOUTHCOM's best bet was to partner with other agencies and governments in the southern hemisphere to mitigate and meliorate the violence, instability, and suffering in the region. Our top priorities revolved around collaborating with others to counter transnational threat networks, preparing for and responding to crises and disasters, and dealing with external state actors like China and Russia, which were undermining liberal democracy, buoying autocratic governments, and expanding their often-corrupting influence.

We were certainly not going to achieve a breakthrough in the War on Drugs. Nixon began fighting the trade in, and use of, drugs in 1971. All told, the U.S. government has spent a trillion dollars on the effort, attempting to address both the supply and demand sides of the equation.[94] America's appetite for drugs remains insatiable and drug trafficking organizations are ever more resourceful in moving them into the U.S. By the time I joined SOUTHCOM in 2017, the War on Drugs was approaching the half-century mark.

Given our limitations in sensing and interdiction assets, we estimated we could intercept no more than 25% of what we knew was being trafficked via maritime means alone.[95] SOUTHCOM, our interagency colleagues, and international partners could raise the cost of doing business for transnational criminal networks, but we had no real hope of eliminating these resilient, tentacled networks running highly lucrative enterprises. As a sign of our frustration, the major metric used for gauging outcomes was still tons of drugs captured and a number of "foot soldiers" (traffickers) arrested, not the more important metric of how much damage we had done to support networks, kingpins, financiers, and corrupt officials that enabled all the operations.

We also needed deep wells of patience in dealing with the constant shifts in the political fortunes of leaders in the Americas. Our security cooperation projects would slow or stop, or accelerate and sprint, depending on each election cycle. Pervasive corruption, insecurity, and economic struggles in many countries created all too frequent opportunities for the left wing, center, and right-wing factions to rise and fall from power. We saw dramatic leadership and policy shifts in Ecuador and Argentina, for example, that opened prospects for us to re-engage on a variety of sensitive issues. We enhanced counter-trafficking efforts with Quito and helped expose China's state-sponsored Distant Water Fishing fleet that was illicitly fishing in Ecuador's Exclusive Economic Zone, inter alia.

We also strengthened intelligence ties with Argentina and immediately deployed U.S. Navy search and rescue teams to the South Atlantic to assist them in trying to find a lost 32-year diesel submarine with 44 crewmembers onboard. Unfortunately, these actions sometimes only win temporary good will and fleeting moments of deeper cooperation before the next election triggers an elastic snap back into institutional wariness of dealings with the

U.S. Such was the case when leftists returned to power in Buenos Aires in late 2019.

Our greatest test of patience, however, centered on the Venezuela problem. With the largest proven oil reserves on the planet, even exceeding Saudi Arabia, Venezuela for years was known as the richest country in Latin America. Its long descent into a failing petro-state began after leftist Hugo Chavez won the presidency in 1998. His focus on socialist solutions, so-called "Bolivarian missions," to reduce poverty were popular with the working class, but overspending, poor governance, and incompetent management of the nation's oil industry, coupled with plummeting oil prices, sent Venezuela into a death spiral. Chavez grew more authoritarian as did his vice president and successor, Nicolas Maduro, after Chavez died in 2013.

The major geopolitical crisis during my tenure as Director of Intelligence became this metastasizing cancer of Venezuela. The economy and health system had collapsed. Fuel, electricity, and water shortages were pervasive. Hyperinflation was out of control. People suffered from hunger, malnutrition, and disease. Maduro repressed dissent, sanctioned forced evictions, jailed opponents, violently cracked down on street protests, cowed the media, conducted arbitrary arrests, tortured and sexually abused detainees, and engaged in extrajudicial killings. Corrupt senior officials, including military leaders, were actively involved in drug trafficking.[96]

Thousands of ruthless Cuban intelligence and counterintelligence experts spread throughout Maduro's government and security forces helped him keep his grip on power.[97] Russia and China provided arms, loans, and technical assistance, leveraging Venezuela's predicament in pursuit of their own geopolitical and economic objectives. China even shared its "Great Firewall" with Maduro, enabling digital surveillance, internet control, and cyber operations against regime opponents.[98] In these terrifying conditions, it was no surprise that millions of Venezuelans fled the country, creating the second-largest refugee crisis in the world after the Syrian exodus.[99]

From our headquarters in Miami, we patiently worked with the Joint Staff to arrange more surveillance coverage of Venezuela, not just for monitoring the evolving crisis, but to prepare for any contingencies that might require delivery of humanitarian aid or, worse case, evacuation of U.S. citizens. It turned out to be a slow, grinding process to get even a modicum of additional intelligence, surveillance, and reconnaissance support from Washington.

We had hope in early 2019 that Venezuela might finally be saved from tyranny. After Maduro stole the Presidential election from National Assembly opposition leader, Juan Gauido, mass protests grew to hundreds of thousands nationwide. Guaido was recognized by 60 countries, including the U.S., as the rightful president of Venezuela. The popular uprising continued for months despite violent crackdowns. Anticipating the Venezuelan resistance movement might be approaching a threshold moment, SOUTHCOM flew hundreds of tons of food and medical supplies into Curacao and Colombia, pre-staging them to provide needed relief. The acid test event would be Guaido's attempt to lead a convoy carrying these humanitarian supplies across a bridge on the Colombia-Venezuela border near Cucuta in February 2019. Would the Venezuela security forces side with the legitimate president bringing relief supplies to a desperate population, flip en masse to support Guaido, or would the dictatorship prevail by forcibly keeping what Maduro deemed to be a Trojan horse outside his gates?

The hostile clash revealed the answer. Although scores of lower-ranking military members defected, the Venezuelan National Guard and armed "colectivo" gangs turned back the convoy on the bridge using shipping containers and an oil truck, fired tear gas, and torched the lead aid trucks. People power had failed. Security forces bearing lethal instruments, no doubt mindful they could be held accountable for sustained maltreatment of innocent civilians, ultimately decided to protect themselves and their strongman. Guaido's uprising petered out by the spring of 2019.

Maduro's victory was a testament to the ability of authoritarian countries to prop one another up, even against the will of their people. Cuba, Russia, China, Turkey, and Iran all had a hand in prolonging the injustice and oppression perpetrated by the regime in Caracas. As of this writing, Maduro still reigns over the disaster that is modern Venezuela thanks to these anti-democratic external state actors.

As a fundamentally impatient person, I found my time focused on the southern hemisphere the most frustrating two years of my 35-year career. We faced wicked problems with few resources. We encountered a persistent trust deficit associated with America's historical baggage of interventions in Latin America. The U.S. national security community in Washington seemed blind or apathetic regarding the growing degree of influence our strategic competitors (China and Russia) were exerting in the Americas. And notable change, where we could earn it through strengthened partnerships, often proved ephemeral.

The answer, of course, was not to throw up our hands and walk away. The answer was to take the long view, seek whatever support we could muster from inside our own government, and remain a reliable partner with nations in the region. We said our serenity prayers, resigned ourselves to marginal advances, and got to work shaping conditions that could bend the arc of history back toward greater justice and security in our hemisphere.[100] I could no longer just utter empty talk about the need for my country to have strategic patience. I had to personally own it, live it, and find a new level of tolerance for glacial change.

> A leader's emotional control over himself or herself, an ability to self-restrain and calmly let the team do its thing, can become a key determinant of success in any endeavor. Impatience often leads to rushed or arbitrary deadlines that can breed septic stress that interferes more than it contributes to team productivity.

> Each organization has a maximum sustainable cadence as it strives to reach new heights. Leaders must figure out their unit's maximum rpm zone and avoid redlining unless conditions truly demand it.

> Leaders must stay tuned in to unexpected difficulties and unintended consequences no one could have imagined from the start because those realities will necessitate smart adjustments to original guidance. They must take deep breaths themselves to let the organization itself breathe.

> Radical efforts to rush history can generate extreme resistance and often backfire. Lasting and hopeful change often requires thousands of encouragements over time.

43

RISK

"Only those who dare to fail greatly can ever achieve greatly."

– Robert F. Kennedy

I was riddled with shyness growing up. I shrank from group gatherings, preferring to hang out on the fringes, observing but not engaging. This held true at school, on sports teams, or at family get-togethers. As a Navy brat, we moved around often enough for me to lose any friends I may have managed to make, usually just a handful of other quiet kids. I was generally introverted with people, "in my head" as the saying goes, yet extroverted for adventure, happiest in nature, exploring new places, and thrilled to discover what was over the next hill or around the next street corner. Left to my own devices, I created my own worlds, fueled largely by my favorite authors like C. S. Lewis, Rudyard Kipling, J. R. R. Tolkien, Jules Verne, and Jack London. This was my portable talent, weaving myself and my imaginative inventions into my new surroundings, which I could take anywhere we ended up.

Reader's Digest, which I religiously consumed through my middle school years, turned me around. In the Quotable Quotes section, one anonymous author had written "Many a man is praised for his reserve when he is simply too proud to risk making a fool of himself." I read and reread the quote. It struck me how true this was for me— the description had me dead to rights. At that very moment, I vowed to change, to be less prideful and more courageous in life. I dedicated myself to favoring engagement over disengagement. It started with simple things like raising my hand and asking questions in class, which I had been loath to do for years.

By the time I became a naval officer, I was more practiced and comfortable taking risks. I had developed a strong independent streak in my youth, a byproduct of being on my own a lot and learning to trust myself. I now possessed a drive to engage and pursue what I thought was worthy of being pursued, even when it didn't conform to conventional wisdom. In that vein, the most significant career decision I made as a young lieutenant was to study Asia, China in particular. Asia was forecasted to be the epicenter of the global economy in the 21st century, our engine of future growth. My very first graded briefing in intelligence school as an officer covered the shocking Tiananmen Square massacre in Beijing in June 1989. If the Chinese Communist Party was this ruthless to run over its own people with tanks and machine gun students down, this unwilling to offer additional freedoms to its people, this anti-democratic and authoritarian, yet growing more powerful by the day due to its incredible economic boom, then the world was about to face another rising power with a different conception of how the world should operate. China was on the path to replacing Russia as the next major power that would challenge the West and the international order. I chose to prioritize understanding China matters, even though it was not viewed as career-enhancing in the mid-1990s.

In subsequent years, I dove deeper to learn more. Where other officers diversified their career portfolios and fought for various hot jobs that would make them promotable as fast as possible, I sequenced five jobs in a row that dealt mainly with China issues. Like our naval intelligence community role model, Edwin Layton, who built Japanese experience before World War II and helped turn the tide in the Pacific War against the Imperial Navy, I was

accruing compound interest in my China experience base.[101] As
the only Mandarin speaker, I led a group of three other officers
throughout China for weeks of area and cultural familiarization in
1999. I joined a high-level Navy team in Taiwan to officially evaluate the Republic of China's Navy in 2000. Admiral Denny Blair, the
Indo-Pacific Commander, invited me to accompany him on a trip
to China to help restart military-to-military talks with the People's
Liberation Army. I was involved as a red team leader in a host of
war games, modeling, exercises, and planning events in the Pacific
theater. I also helped bring our joint contingency and operations
plans up to snuff. Later in Washington, I was put in charge of advocating for major Navy programs related to China in the Quadrennial
Defense Review.

In taking these jobs, I strayed significantly from the normal
career tracks of my peers and ran the risk of becoming a "one trick
pony." However I felt the hazards of becoming a maverick specialist were outweighed by the importance of developing substantive
knowledge on what I thought would become our top intelligence
challenge, especially for our Navy. I also realized that I needed to
take increasing risks in vocalizing what I knew of coming dangers.
It was insufficient to develop expertise and simply be in the know.
Insights had to be communicated to those with enough power to do
something about the magnifying problems of China's rapid military
modernization and assertive foreign policy.

Of course, after 9/11, it became instantly unpopular to discuss
the potency of formative China threats. The defense department
(rightly) needed to devote more time, resources, and energy to the
Global War on Terror. After all, it was the closest wolf to the sled and
religious extremists were planning to do more harm to Americans
from their sanctuaries in the Middle East. But we couldn't boresight
solely on radical Muslims. A number of us tried to warn the Navy
of increasingly capable anti-ship ballistic missiles that China was
developing, for instance. For too long these significant threats were
pooh-poohed and downplayed by disbelieving scientists, acquisition

professionals, warfare officers, and policymakers, losing us years in developing counters. With dread, I witnessed the growing risk of inaction by my Service and the larger Defense Department.

As I became senior and more involved in high-level "star chambers," the stakes rose decidedly higher. Hawks in Beijing were hell-bent on pursuing their ambitions with the comprehensive national power of a juggernaut. We were now dealing with a peer competitor in almost every respect. I became significantly more outspoken about inadequately addressed threats and dangers. There was no shy-kid fiber left in my body anymore. The consequences of ignorance and passivity were too dire. In countless meetings with senior admirals and generals, civilian officials, members of Congress, and even journalists (at the unclassified level), I delivered inconvenient truths about Chinese threats. Along with a small team of other China experts, we spoke up at every chance, in every message, at every conference, and in every session discussing China. We received plenty of pushback from doubters who thought we had more time to deal with certain issues; however, we stuck to our guns and pushed back equally hard, patiently laying out the intelligence and the strategic context for leaders who had more Middle East than Asia experience. Some of these interactions got testy, because our intelligence implied that the U.S. needed to do more than it was doing, forcing hard tradeoff decisions.

It took years, for example, to convince the Chairman of the Joint Chiefs of Staff of the rising possibility of Chinese aggression against Taiwan in the 2020s, not the 2030s or 2040s. I remember sitting behind General Milley during one of his first visits to Hawaii. Admiral Phil Davidson, the Combatant Commander, was delivering a theater briefing in his office using a wall-size map of the Indo-Pacific. Our senior staff was always invited to listen to the discussion and contribute where appropriate. The Chairman expressed skepticism about any major Chinese actions for quite some time, drawing a parallel to the incredible difficulties of U.S. forces defeating entrenched Japanese forces on small islands during World War II. I glanced at Admiral Davidson, who gave me a nod, and I offered out loud that the best historical parallel from World War II was probably Operation Husky in 1943 when the Allies conducted an amphibious assault on Sicily, which was defended by mainly Italians with only a couple German divisions. Ugly, but doable. The Chinese might be tempted to take action if we didn't do anything to change the current dynamics.

Ultimately our National Security Strategy proclaimed that the 2020s were the "decisive decade" in shaping the strategic competition with China. The document helped stimulate more action and greater investments in the Indo-Pacific than ever before. The national security establishment had awakened not to just see the danger, but resolved to do something about it.

Looking back, I willingly assumed career risks to learn about China, then assumed more career risks to communicate about China to others. Many other intelligence analysts did so as well. Few senior leaders want to hear consistently bad news or face the difficulties of having to undertake herculean action to address major shortfalls. In that environment, it can be tempting to shoot the messenger. Yet absent risk-taking to get people's attention, organizations and even countries can end up walking backward into costly surprises. Someone's got to stick their neck out and shoot the right message. I felt I have enlarged my life, learning, and relevance by taking calculated risks. In fact, I believe striving for the greater good actually demands it of us, even if we may be shy at heart.

> The more senior one gets, the more risk-astute one should be. Risk is a muscle that will strengthen from repeated use. It also can injure from overuse.

> Excessive fear of uncertainty will interfere with one's ability to enlarge one's life, learning, and relevance.[102]

> The risk of inaction in many cases can be more dangerous than the risk of action. Self-paralysis exercised often enough can become the prison bars we build around ourselves.

> Failures of moral courage and passive spectating aren't just a form of disengagement but a potentially consequential exercise in irresponsibility.

> Smart risk-takers are more likely to create their own luck and be rewarded professionally than those who seek safety first and foremost. Learn to thread the zone between phantom fears and foolish risks because no great challenge or reward ever yields to timidity.

44

PERFORMANCE
AND MORALE

"Outstanding leaders go out of their way
to boost the self-esteem of their personnel.
If people believe in themselves, it's amazing
what they can accomplish."

– Sam Walton

It is a false conception among inexperienced people that the harder you push your people the lower you will drive morale. Most people do hard. Most people are motivated by worthy challenges. It's true that "when the going gets tough, the tough get going." The caveat is that if you treat your people like automatons, sooner or later they will abandon ship.

Ineffective leaders slave drive. They are all rigor, all the time. Effective leaders employ rigor, but they enlist the heart as well. They know that people need to feel valued beyond the immediate contributions they provide. Workers need ready relief in the workplace and enrichment in their lives that goes beyond their primary tasking, even if they are passionate about their tasking. If you want quality of *service* from subordinates, leaders must improve their quality of *life* at work. Something beyond pay, compensation packages, stock options, and health plans.

We will return to the Office of Naval Intelligence as a case study. As an enterprise, ONI was not living up to its full potential and its reputation in key circles was suffering. Production across subordinate analytic centers was uneven and quality standards varied. Analytic pieces were commonly lengthy and late. Too many were narrow, highly specialized, hyper detailed. Although ONI was quick to answer requests for information, ONI's general analytic production process was so dilatory that other agencies like the Defense Intelligence Agency and Central Intelligence Agency regularly scooped it. Worse, many senior decision-makers were rarely reading ONI's intelligence—even naval intelligence officers building daily read books for admirals and joint leaders would scarcely select them.[103] ONI, by default, was ceding its responsibility to serve as the premier agency for maritime intelligence. It was not always the ready authoritative voice on any global maritime issue of consequence.[104]

My predecessor, Rear Admiral Curt Copley, had already collaborated with the workforce to architect the most sweeping reorganization at ONI since 2009. Adjustments were designed to make ONI fit for a new era of strategic competition. I pulled the trigger on those renovation plans when I arrived in 2022, which would address some underlying issues at hand. But more was required. ONI needed to get back to the basics of emphasizing consistently high-quality output, tighter connectedness with its primary partners and clients, and improved accessibility of its deliverables.

So, on top of a convulsive renovation shift affecting major elements in our enterprise, I set down new demands to address the above shortfalls. I explained the need for additional course corrections and we embarked on an array of the solutions that required even more of the workforce. Our high-stakes mission support required it, especially in light of high-visibility maritime developments such as the Black Sea maritime conflict and grain shipment drama in the Ukraine War, China's intensifying belligerence with maritime assets in the Western Pacific, the PLA's introduction of new weapons and platforms, Iranian harassment and attacks on merchant shipping in the Middle East, North Korea's development of new maritime ballistic and cruise missiles, Russia's long-range surface and submarine deployments to within weapons range of the U.S., Russia's testing of advanced superweapons, the list went on.

That's the stuff we pursued with our heads. Now what to do with the heart to buoy morale? Of course, our reward system was wired for sound. In addition to time off, monetary spot awards, and medals, we added monthly "Masters of Excellence" awards for Quality, Connectedness, and Accessibility (the areas where we needed to improve). We would showcase the people who earned recognition and ask them to share their stories. Usually, we would then transition into our so-called Knowledge 360 TED-talk sessions. The vibe during these shindigs was always upbeat.

We also started an Admiral's Cup competition. Eight different commands in the National Maritime Intelligence Center complex out at Suitland, Maryland would compete for points and a winner would be crowned at the end of the year. Unlike other military bases, however, which ran cups focused exclusively on athletic events, we encouraged as many people as possible from the workforce to get involved by adding a patchwork quilt of talent tests. We allowed the workforce to nominate and vote on their favorite events, which led us to include chess, Connect 4, ping pong, bowling, a chili cook-off, karaoke mirrored on "The Voice," and (yes, this was an intelligence command after all) Jeopardy Intelligence and Dungeons & Dragons.

The talent contests were morale-boosters, even more so when command leaders circulated during the events, participating or encouraging their folks on the sidelines. I was out there for the 5Ks, got whooped at Pickle Ball, and had more than my fair share of dodge balls bounced off my chest. Stories and photos, along with other professional articles, would be included in our internal rag, the ONI Intelligencer.

Parking, on the other hand, was the single greatest morale killer of the ONI workforce. A multi-story garage near our compound had to be torn down due to cracking concrete years earlier than antici-pated. The replacement lot was under construction and unusable for over a year, forcing a third of the workforce to park far off the compound. As soon as I got there, I took trips on the shuttle with my command master chief to understand the logistical headaches. I regularly gave out my commander's parking pass for my space near the front entrance. Noticing the curved drive in front of the building for VIP flagpole parking was unused for long stretches, I asked our facilities team to paint new marked spaces there. These efforts didn't substantially change the parking nightmare, but they demonstrated that leadership was doing everything in their power to help address their greatest dissatisfier.

We engaged in a host of other projects to address quality of life, from adding game boards in our corporate agora in the skylit lunch area to placing TVs in high-trafficked building intersections that would play educational and informational videos, including short selfie video messages I would record to the workforce when out and about on my external engagements. We also bought more books for our small library, best of the best works on a variety of topics, then set up a "Books on the Bridge Wing" display near a major employee entrance to increase the ease with which people could check out professionally useful, non-fiction titles. On alternating weeks, I would send out four "Quotable Quotes" or a "Leadership Minute" to all hands.

Of course, one of the best ways to add heart to an organization is simply stopping by and asking how people are doing. My walkabouts were the highlight of my day and I know people appreciated being seen and listened to. Circulations among the workforce are critical to know and be known, for people to feel connected with their leaders, and to open oneself up to absorb any slings and arrows that the chain of command might deserve. Good leaders know that unfamiliarity actually breeds contempt.

The day before I turned over the Office of Naval Intelligence to another admiral and prepared to retire, I passed a senior civilian analyst who worked in the Kennedy Maritime Analysis Center, one of ONI's subordinate commands. He walked by with a courteous greeting then a second later turned around, "Hey Admiral, got a sec?" "Of course, always," I said. "Before you leave I just wanted to say thanks for riding the fine line between being a disruptor and inspiring people around here. I know it's hard to oversee change and demand improvements and still maintain good morale, but somehow you made it work." I thanked him and turned with a little glow in my own heart. Inspiration can be delivered both up as well as down.

The greatest imperative for a leader is to achieve maximum performance at the highest morale in their organization. These mutually inclusive, symbiotic end states demand everything a leader can give—a lavish commitment of brainpower and frequent doses of heart and soul. Picking one over the other is a false choice, and usually results in a team only ever becoming half as good as its real potential.

> Coached with rigor and heart, nothing is stronger than skilled professionals in possession of genuine team spirit.

> Horsewhipping a unit into shape can garner a short-term performance benefit through scare tactics, but does nothing to win hearts and minds. At the other extreme, one can excessively accommodate to try to please and win the loyalty of subordinates—a common junior leader mistake—but that path ultimately saps the unit's discipline. A balanced firm, but fair approach forms the best substratum to grow capable, high-integrity organizations.

> Organizations rarely sustain peak performance and tip-top morale. The output and moods of any organization oscillate. It's a leader's job is to work at all times to create updrafts.

> Leaders that endeavor to elevate performance and morale to the highest attainable net average are better able to channel energies at critical moments when circumstances demand an organization perform at its very best.

45

CHANGE

"Don't be fooled by the calm. That's always the time to change course—not when you're just about to get hit by a typhoon."

– Thomas Friedman

Change resistors push back in overt and covert ways. The larger the scope of change, the more the status quo snipers scope you into their crosshairs. But you don't get traction without friction, as they say. For a senior officer, you know you will spark bureaucratic battles when you dare new things. Heck, promotions come with an acknowledgment that you've acquired jujitsu-like infighting skills and the accompanying judgment to know when, and when not, to use them.

My senior intelligence team in the Pacific deserves credit for knowing it was time to step up as change agents. Starting in late 2019, we began advocating for improvements to our information capabilities at the Indo-Pacific Command (INDOPACOM) and, by extension, the Department of Defense and Intelligence Community. Typically, nations that best advance their national security and economic prospects use so-called DIME instruments of national power: Diplomatic, Information, Military, and Economic measures.[105] Ideally, all four are used robustly and smartly, independently, and/or integrated as needed to achieve desired effects. Our information instrument, however, was not firing on all cylinders in dealing with the nation's

#1 challenge: China. It was not unfair to judge America's information game as anemic.

Unfortunately, China was running circles around us in terms of energetically and proactively using its information instrument to flood global media outlets with its prompt and polished narratives. Beijing cast itself as a champion for globalization, a model of effective governance, achiever of economic miracles. It touted its "peaceful rise" as it proclaimed it would move into the center stage of the world, bringing peace, stability, and non-interference in other nations' sovereign matters. Confucius Institutes throughout the world touted China's peaceful DNA and inherent benevolence. China promised connectivity, progress, and prosperity through its Belt and Road Initiative. It loaned capital, and struck infrastructure and access deals for ports, rail systems, and airfield development. It sold its information technology abroad at bottom basement prices. It pushed its language of "digital sovereignty," "development as a human right," and a "community for common destiny for mankind," successfully insinuating its priorities into the United Nations and other international bodies.[106]

Simultaneously, China proclaimed liberal democracies were inefficient and ineffective in dealing with modern challenges. They contrasted China's successes with the West's failures. They pointed out previous financial crises in the West, its checkered economic performance, Brexit, poor early management of the COVID pandemic, growth of chauvinistic populists, and intensifying internal divisions within democracies that produced gridlock, concluding that the "East is rising, the West is declining."[107]

China assailed Western alliances as anachronistic, promoting a "Cold War mindset" that aimed to break the world into adversarial blocs. It described the U.S. as unfit to lead in the global community because it was the "black hand" behind every color revolution that left countries in chaos. America was painted as the most dangerous and destabilizing force on the planet, prone to violent aggression that, for example, produced profound suffering in the Middle East in its misguided attempts to exert hegemony. America and its allies were cast as untrustworthy, exploitative, and unable to handle even their own domestic problems. Beijing also claimed U.S. military operations in the Pacific were provocative and disruptive, conceived only to encircle and contain China, and stop its rise.

Harping on these themes, China's propaganda machine continued to churn out largely unchallenged narratives to gain increasingly more "discourse power," as they called it, essentially state-based political work designed to reshape global perceptions, values, and concepts. The intent was to elevate China into the position as the strongest, wisest voice on acceptable norms in the 21st century, ultimately making the world safe for authoritarianism and enabling China to re-attain what it deemed to be its rightful place at the top of the modern multipolar system.[108]

While China curated itself as a responsible stakeholder and righteous leader in the international system, the reality was starkly different. China routinely interfered in the domestic politics of many nations, coopting political and business elites through weaponized corruption and other influence operations. They carried out pervasive espionage and information operations, enabled by United Front Work Department activities, using their embassies, consulates, friendship societies, Confucius Institutes, student associations on college campuses, businessmen, and other entities to achieve leverage over power centers in other countries. Chinese information and communications technology companies, enabled by state subsidies to sell cheap networks abroad in high volume, inked global contracts and then shared data passing through those networks with Chinese intelligence services. What data China couldn't get through those means, they stole through widespread and persistent cyber hacking operations designed to abscond intellectual property, especially technology secrets, of other nations.[109]

China routinely failed to live up to basic agreements, like World Trade Organization rules and the U.N. Convention on the Law of the Sea. It used its maritime militia, China Coast Guard, and Navy to

coerce and bully in areas where Beijing asserted illegal, extraterritorial claims. China unleashed the People's Liberation Army and its
other security services to pressure its neighbors. China was even able
to set up its own police stations in other countries to help discipline
expat Chinese communities and capture dissidents.[110]

Meanwhile, at home in mainland China, the true character of the
Chinese Communist Party manifested in increasingly totalitarian
policies and tightened controls over their population. Oppression ran
rampant. The combination of complete digital dominance behind the
Great Firewall, ubiquitous surveillance cameras, expansive security
apparatus, and social credit score system engineered an environment
surpassing any Orwellian dystopian nightmare. Xi Jinping demanded
new forms of ideological conformity as he reasserted the primacy of
the Party. Freedom of thought was quashed, Party opponents were
imprisoned, Uyghurs were rounded up in detention and re-education
camps in Xinjiang, religious organizations were persecuted, and the
State increasingly clamped down on the private sector.[111]

Unfortunately, China's influence was also so pervasive in America
that it dampened our ability to have open conversations within
our own country about the true nature of the Chinese problem.
Our economies were intertwined. Hollywood and the U.S. business
community had been hushed because they were beholden to Chinese
markets and distribution networks. Venture capitalists continued
to see promise in investing in cutting-edge Chinese start-ups. U.S.
academia depended on Chinese tuition dollars. Companies under-
played their victimization by Chinese cyber actors and exploitation
by Chinese business partners. Our scientific community thought
they couldn't advance without Chinese collaboration. Many politi-
cians saw these dangers and moved out on developing ways to protect
American interests, but few could articulate the breadth and depth
of how dangerous China had become to our society—our values,
prosperity, and security.

For all these reasons, China was able to continue to exercise
a free hand in advancing its mercantilist policies, deepening its

penetration of other nations, and eroding America's standing in the world. Although many pundits discounted the power of China's information activities, in fact, Beijing's messages strongly resonated in the Global South, where many Third World countries genuinely aligned with China's perspectives. Many small to mid-size countries felt burned or neglected by First World powers. They trusted Beijing, eagerly took Chinese loans, deepened their bilateral relationships, and allowed China almost unfettered access to their societies. An alarming number of countries in Europe and the West were also walking down this primrose path, naïve or willfully ignoring the true intentions of the leaders in Beijing. Too many countries were making purely short-term economic choices, blind to the mid- to long-term implications to their security and sovereignty.

It was against this backdrop that we realized, at least in our theater, that INDOPACOM needed to do a better job exposing Chinese ambitions, stratagems, and malign behavior. We needed to assist in puncturing false narratives and correcting distortions continually spewing from Beijing. We need to wage the truth. Our databases were thick with intelligence evidence of wrongdoing, specific ways China was undermining the international order, how they were penetrating other societies, the Machiavellian methods they used to advance their ambitions, and what they were trying to accomplish. While we shared some of this intelligence directly with our allies and partners, little effort was being made in the public domain to call China out. Many of us were not surprised by this debility. After all, America's public diplomacy efforts during the Global War Terror left a lot to be desired.

I walked into the 4-star Commander's office at INDOPACOM headquarters to propose we send a requirements memo to the Director of National Intelligence to help address the problem. Admiral Phil Davidson and I had worked together previously when he was Carrier Strike Group Eight's Commander and I was his senior intelligence officer (N2). He was a former military aide to the vice president and at that point the longest-serving Surface Warfare Officer in the Navy, earning him the sobriquet "Old Salt." He was a towering figure and

a strategic thinker. We sat at his table with long windows overlook-
ing Pearl Harbor and the USS *Arizona* Memorial. The view from the
hills of Camp Smith of the watery tomb of 1,102 sailors and marines
served as a constant reminder of our duty. For intelligence officers,
in particular, it was a ghostly call from a tragic past to warn better of
dangers to America and to do so in time to make a difference.

Admiral Davidson fully supported the proposal to ask the
Intelligence Community to both downgrade select classified material
and produce more material at the unclassified level to provide ammu-
nition for U.S. messaging, aka information "fires." He agreed with
the general philosophy that omniscient spectating—knowing what's
happening and remaining voiceless or vacuous with our messaging
to international audiences—wasn't the right way to strategically
compete. We needed more purposeful action to connect the dots for
others, warn with evidence, and motivate beneficiaries of the international rules-based system to better protect it from threats posed
by authoritarian spoilers. To defend a free and open Indo-Pacific, we
need the proof and authoritativeness that could only come from our
Intelligence Community.

I authored a two-page memo to the Director of National
Intelligence, outlining the challenges and articulating the need
to expose both Chinese and Russian malign actions. At Admiral
Davidson's encouragement, we coordinated with other Combatant
Command J2s to see if their four-star bosses wanted to co-sign. Nine
of eleven Combatant Commanders eventually did so, an extremely
rare occurrence. The missive became popularly known as the "36-star
Memo" and was quickly endorsed by the Director of National
Intelligence. It started the ball rolling on reviewing intelligence policies and procedures, ultimately squeezing a little more output than
before. But in a testament to cultural resistance, some intelligence
agencies viewed production at the unclassified level, even in small
amounts, as anathema. Select improvements were appreciated where
they occurred, but many agencies remained reactive and leery, offering only token cooperation.[112]

At INDOPACOM, we couldn't wait for the Intelligence Community to realize we could lose the battle of the narratives and lose the peace with strategic competitors like China if we continued to treat the public swath of the information domain as unimportant. Our team saw continuous missed opportunities to correct falsehoods and we watched with chagrin as U.S. messaging continued to be late, weak, or plain absent.

So, I directed a special analytic team composed of some of our best China experts to show how it could be done. They started producing unclassified intelligence papers that could support our theater information teams. The papers were pulled from open sources using classic source vetting and fusion techniques to highlight ground truth on an array of Chinese pernicious activities. We gradually enriched those papers with downgraded intelligence, where sources and methods could be easily obfuscated. It took over a year to work through bureaucratic resistance to these papers in Washington. We had produced 50 of those papers by the time I left INDOPACOM a couple of years later. They were all enthusiastically shared with our foreign counterparts by INDOPACOM, other Combatant Commands, multiple government agencies, and many embassies. Several presidents and prime ministers in theater ultimately decided to keep China out of sensitive areas of their countries based on these factual and persuasive intelligence papers. We had figured out an effective way of unshackling the truth to contest Chinese disinformation.

It was no surprise to us in the middle of the Pacific that change of this magnitude was going to be an uphill battle in Washington. My team remained confident that our ideas about how the Intelligence Community in the 21st century needed to perform more proficiently at delivering at all levels of classification—Top Secret compartmented to unclassified—would eventually take root. As with all change, what is originally regarded as revolutionary eventually becomes conventional wisdom. Innovators bring in early adopters, the majority slowly comes around, then laggards come last. Major change across reluctant bureaucracies is typically measured in years, not months, to be sure.

It was encouraging to see released intelligence finally used effectively as an instrument of national power during Russia's invasion of Ukraine in 2022. Selective disclosures work when we do it right. As of this writing, momentum has also built in strengthening our information instrument in dealing with China. Change agents know that the pressure is always greatest at the point where you are creating a bow wave, but it's the only way to ultimately get on plane and speed into a new sea of possibilities.

> Any organization that wishes to remain relevant in a fast-paced, ever-shifting world must remain open to renovating itself.[113]

> Modern challenges require us to collectively possess an opportunity mindset—a willingness to relentlessly hunt for leverage—even if that sometimes means painful adjustments to structures, processes, and approaches.

> Fluidity of change requires more people who are "virtuosos of the moment" and "masters of the passing instant" willing to make small-scale adjustments on the fly, or larger ones if macro-dynamics veer.[114]

> Innovation *in action* takes organizations to new heights; innovation *inaction* sinks even the best-intentioned enterprises.

> Smart upgrades, so long as they can quickly re-establish stability in a more productive norm, can free teams to reallocate their energies away from lower-calorie work to more consequential activities.

46

FARSIGHTEDNESS

*"If a man does not know to what port he
is steering, no wind is favorable."*

– Seneca

"A dapt or die" is sometimes not too strong a capture of the imperative to take charge of changing one's circumstances before they are dramatically and deleteriously changed by others. I saw this first-hand at a macro level in dealing with a potential major power conflict over Taiwan.

Taiwan is one of several flashpoints in the Pacific, one that is deemed most likely to bring superpowers to blows. Since taking power in 2012, General Secretary Xi Jinping in Beijing has prioritized resolving the political status of Taiwan as part of China's self-declared dream. He is on record declaring China's rejuvenation cannot be achieved without Taiwan's assimilation under Chinese Communist Party (CCP) rule before 2049. Xi has said all his life's accomplishments will have been a failure if Taiwan is not unified on his watch. Xi has rejected the pre-existing wisdom of earlier Chinese leaders, who were prepared to wait many years to resolve the Taiwan problem given the complexities and disaster likely to follow any unilateral attempt to change the status quo.[115]

China's sweeping military build-up over the last 25 years has been designed with an invasion contingency in mind, with prodigious warfare investments designed to conquer Taiwan and defeat any "interventionist" powers that might come to Taiwan's rescue, whether they be the U.S., Japan, Australia, or any others. China would prefer to achieve political unification without resorting to combat as they follow Sun Tzu's teachings that "to subdue the enemy without fighting is the acme of skill." But Beijing's increasing use of coercive military pressure has increased the risk of sparking outright conflict. Xi has also mandated that the People's Liberation Army (PLA) accelerate key modernization goals for 2027, and is making every preparation for war, which has sent cold shivers through the region. The rapid growth of China's war machine, coupled with extraterritorial claims, rampant bullying tactics, and threatening rhetoric, has become the single most destabilizing trend in the Indo-Pacific.

Along with many others at the Indo-Pacific Command, I was asked to step into this dangerous milieu to help Taiwan transform itself in ways that would deter China from resorting to violence to fulfill Xi's ambitions. Taiwan would have to take charge of its destiny, strengthen its capabilities, and transform, or its fate would surely be sealed by ardent revanchists in Beijing. Taiwan had seen how the CCP exploited lawfare and crackdowns to crush freedom and end promised autonomy in Hong Kong. Taiwan's citizens had been awakened to the reality that they faced a similar, potentially more imminent existential threat than previously imagined.

I visited Taiwan three times in my capacity as director of intelligence, building on other visits I had made to Taiwan years earlier as a more junior officer. I ended up being the first active duty two-star flag/general officer to visit Taiwan in more than 40 years, ever since we abrogated our Mutual Defense Treaty with Taiwan in favor of diplomatic recognition of Beijing. I conducted battlefield circulation, re-familiarizing myself with Taiwan's terrain, standing defenses, and war plans. Taiwan's military leaders appreciated my candid thoughts on adversary challenges and options for strengthening their force posture.

My last two visits were directed by the Office of the Secretary of Defense and National Security Council. Based on the goodwill I had earned during my first visit, I was tasked in 2021 to brief President Tsai on the Chinese invasion threat. I was flown in with just one other colleague for a low-profile nighttime landing, secreted to a hotel, and shuttled back and forth to the Presidential Palace for two straight days of briefings to the President, cabinet officials, defense leaders, intelligence seniors, and other policy advisors. We reviewed the correlation of forces, the increased dangers presented by the PLA, and all the ways China was readying its forces to harm Taiwan.

The President and her leadership team were highly appreciative of the briefings and detailed discussions. President Tsai commented, "I've waited four years for a brief like this!" The Chinese were not so appreciative. As our plane departed to the northeast from Taipei through international airspace back to Hawaii, the pilot asked me to come up to the cockpit. Two PLA Navy warships on patrol in the East China Sea were repeatedly calling out: "U.S. aircraft, you are in Chinese airspace. Leave now!" The brazen radio intimidation in the international commons reminded me of how dangerous China's rise was becoming. The U.S., our allies, and many international partners would have to find more effective ways to protect freedom, democracy, and the international system that China intended to gradually coopt and undermine as it used its strengthening powers to advance its national objectives at the expense of others.

A few months after Russia invaded Ukraine in 2022, I was directed back to Taipei to brief President Tsai and her team on wartime lessons that Taiwan should factor as they prepared to deal with all forms of Chinese aggression. By that time, Taiwan was already on the path to developing additional asymmetric capabilities, extending its conscription service length, and mobilizing its population to blend civil and military capabilities to effect a People's War defense of the island, if necessary. President Tsai was thinking through resilience issues and paid close attention to specific lessons that enabled

Ukraine, a supposedly inferior power, to stop a superior invader from attaining a quick victory, or any real benefit from its naked aggression. President Tsai called the brief "marvelous, comprehensive, and a checklist for Taiwan" as she evaluated additional society-wide defense improvements. At the end, she strode past all the COVID plexiglass partitions that divided us in the Presidential briefing room and bumped elbows with me.

Taiwan's predicament reminds us that becoming a captain of one's destiny and master of one's fate involves hard choices. Whether dealing with personal concerns, organizational issues, or international affairs, farsighted leaders exercise their capacity to make change on their terms before chance first defines choices for them. They confront the brutal facts of their existence while maintaining confidence in their power to overcome adversity and uncertainty.[116] They possess a vision and faith in their ability to realize a better future. They own an outlook that is more karma than kismet, a belief that purposeful deeds and actions possess powerful agency to shape the future. It's the equivalent of confidently taking the helm and steering by a worthy polestar, no matter the sea state, nor how long it might take to arrive on the far horizon.

➤ The future is not linear or strictly evolutionary. It is often defined by unexpected fractures and jumps.[117] Uncertainties abound, improbabilities emerge, and surprise strikes; therefore, flexibility and adaptability must become a leader's watchwords.

➤ One of the best forms of flexibility involves shaping the environment and people around us instead of waiting for circumstances and others to sweep us away.[118]

➤ Foresight requires keeping an eye on weather developing on far horizons.[119] You must not just steer away from danger but aim for promising destinations.

➤ Farsightedness isn't predicting the future, it's imagining what it can be and making speed toward it. It's about acting instead of being acted upon.

WHY LEADERSHIP
REALLY MATTERS

We face a crisis of leadership in America today. None of us should be content with where our society stands in terms of leadership performance in recent years. Though impossible to measure, our generation seems to be seeing more than its fair share of flawed leaders exerting influence over our country. As a result, excessive dysfunction and fragmentation bridle our nation. Enough leaders with rust-encrusted integrity, who somehow never learned or failed to consistently apply many of the leadership principles outlined in this book, have kinked our chain and weighed down our true potential.

America is remarkably resilient and I am optimistic about our continuing potential as a country, but we will not be at our best unless we rededicate ourselves, individually and collectively, to improve who we are as leaders. We must demand more of ourselves and we must demand more of our fellow citizens.

Leading well is the quintessential source of American excellence, the indispensable virtue that has enabled greatness in our land. We still enjoy many superb leaders in all sectors of society, but in too many places leadership is starting to become a neglected and undervalued skill. Fewer people we can respect and admire, who we want to unquestionably trust, are taking us forward into the future. We are longing for our generation's greats, the heroes of our age, who we hope would be humble, foresighted, and wise. We yearn for those who could bring out the best in us, inspire us, unite us despite our differences. We ache for people in power to do the right things for the right reasons, and always the right way.

Unfortunately, history shows us societies can easily be brought down by too many "misleaders" in positions of power, whose abilities, bearing, judgment, allegiances, or morality were stunted somewhere along the line. We cannot afford to be brought low by unfit people inside our country, especially at a time when external enemies are actively seeking to undermine American power and influence. The stakes for our nation are higher than most American citizens seem to realize. Nothing short of our security, values, freedoms, and prosperity are on the line. We need to lose our inattention blindness and awaken to the serious predicament we are in.

Most notably, our self-destructive politics has given oxygen for adversaries like the Chinese Communist Party, now leading the second-most powerful nation on earth, to strengthen their comprehensive national power and global influence by contrasting it with the polarization, chaos, inwardness, and gridlock of America's democracy. China, Russia, and confederates like Iran and North Korea are well on their way to executing their grand strategies to reshape the world according to their preferences. Surging cases of coercion and outright aggression show they are willing to use almost any means to do so. These autocrats sense opportunity because America's political shenanigans and chronic leadership gaffes make us look institutionally feeble. Too many American leaders blithely continue to prioritize power, party, and partisanship over common sense compromise, country, and the Constitution. Tyranny exists in our time, its breath is on our necks from foreign powers, and it is actually growing within our body politic.

Intensified high-stakes geopolitics, state-sponsored aggression, globalization backsliding, economic de-risking, climate change disasters, pandemic threats, resource depletion, population stresses, persistent cyber threats, organized crime, and the continuing realities of terrorism in our time require that we act with greater velocity and togetherness than ever before.

I am convinced that American innovation, creativity, and openness remain our national strengths and we possess the inherent stamina and grit to deal with any domestic or international challenges, but internecine conflicts engineered domestically by blinkered leaders have become our Achilles Heel. We need to get out of our own way. More to the point, we must hold our current leaders accountable for better outcomes, ones that reflect the true will and needs of the people, or move the recalcitrant aside by starving them of positions, attention, funding, votes, or any other means of support they depend on. We need to remove the weakest links that keep dividing our chains and replace them with people made of better stuff. In doing so, we will restore honor, integrity, and respect to all our proceedings, and rediscover the spirit of cooperation that made us a truly great nation to begin with.

What does right look like? Right looks like restoration of public trust in institutions to perform their core functions properly. Right looks like effective, empowering, and fair representation and governance for all citizens.[120] Right looks like neither tyranny of the majority nor tyranny of the minority in our democracy. Right looks like persistent honesty and upstanding behavior from those in positions of authority in every sector of our society. Right looks like companies upholding principles of business ethics. Right looks like media professionals distinguishing facts from opinion or rhetoric. Right looks like a diverse citizenry exercising patience, understanding, and empathy toward people born of different circumstances. Right looks like communities looking out for one another. Right looks like people minding their manners and disagreeing agreeably. Right looks like individuals striving to be a source of inspiration for all with whom they come in contact. And right looks like a nation that looks up, sees the multiple storms on the horizon, and realizes it is time to row together in unison for the preservation of all they should be holding dear.

Our national crisis persists because we are growing numb to what is wrong around us. But I have not lost hope. I spent 35 years of my life in the cloth of this country and I've witnessed many people during my time in uniform transform themselves from being the most fragile link in the chain to becoming the main load-bearing node. Led well, I've seen organizations turn around and I've witnessed troubled people wake up to become an enduring source of resonance instead of dissonance in their environment.[121]

So, I believe we can change and we can be better. It's just time for more Americans to believe they must do so. It's time for the true patriots to emerge and become their own form of stainless steel, offering supreme strength, high resistance to life's corrosion and abrasion, and a beauty that reflects light into its world. It's time we interlink better with our fellow citizens who are actually not the real enemy and do our part to lift the great weights of our time.

"On the strength of one link of the cable dependeth the might of the chain" goes the key Law of the Navy, one that applies equally to our nation and world. My hope is every reader internalizes this insight and turns it into a personal clarion call to self-strengthen and interconnect for the greater good. Every citizen should understand the price of freedom is upholding their personal duty to project their best selves into the world, to generate more flex than friction along the master cables of our lives.

Much is at stake. The strains are upon us and we must bear them confidently and with renewed solidarity. It's time to be a link of iron integrity in the mighty chain of our country. And it's time to be leaders who, above all, lift everything in their midst.

ADDITIONAL
LEADERSHIP INSIGHTS

Excerpts and executive synopsis of leadership themes from other sources:

➤ Leadership is inspiring people to do more than they think themselves capable.

➤ Leadership is about doing the right things; management is about doing things right.[122]

➤ Leadership is setting a vision, crafting a plan, getting the right people and resources together, and executing the strategy.

➤ The "vision thing" and planning is relatively easy, execution and follow through is the hard part.

➤ Put first things first, keep the main thing the main thing.[123]

➤ Before acting, take the time to diagnose—deeply understand the problem first.[124]

➤ Be as intentional about what you stop doing as what you start doing.

➤ Avoid jargon and speak in plain English.

➤ Drive out fear—build trust.

➤ Overusing power can derail a leader.[125]

➤ Apply energy that is positive, enlarging, magnifying.[126]

➤ Work with others likely to be affected by any policies or processes you initiate.

➤ Resist the tendency to seek out info that solely supports your view and downplays all else.

➤ Effective people are not problem-oriented, but opportunity-minded.

➤ Leading up and leading across is as important as leading down.

➤ Leadership is enablement in pursuit of a just cause.[127]

➤ Do what you believe, keep pushing to build momentum.[128]

➤ The only constant is change—adapt to thrive.[129]

➤ Align everything to core values.[130]

➤ That extra ounce of commitment, a little more effort, a little longer, can produce breakthrough power.[131]

➤ "It's not just getting results that matter; it's *how* you get the results."[132]

➤ The more sincere and sustained involvement of employees in decisions, the greater the release of everyone's creativity, and a greater commitment to what they create.[133]

➤ Team victory means working together, communicating together, making things happen together.

➤ Leaders must ruthlessly prioritize and relentlessly follow up.

➤ "A player who makes a team great is better than a great player."[134]

➤ "Avoid having your ego so close to your position that when your position falls, your ego goes with it."[135]

➤ Adversity rouses our greatest potential.

➤ "Leadership is wisdom and courage, and a carelessness of self."[136]

ABOUT LEADERS

- Leaders know that brains don't equal rank.[137]

- Leadership involves taking risks.

- The best leaders are ambitious first and foremost for the cause, for the organization, not for himself or herself; and have an absolute iron will to make good on that ambition.[138]

- True leaders have convictions. No one will follow a leader unless they have a belief and value system that guides every decision.

- Leaders are oriented by a strong moral compass, not a weathervane.

- Leaders exercise power to achieve purpose and effect change.[139]

- Leaders connect personal meaning to a higher purpose to create belief and a sense of direction.[140]

- "Great leaders set up their organizations to succeed beyond their own lifetimes."[141]

- Successful leaders "balance pride with humility."[142]

- "Daring leaders model clarity, kindness, and hope."[143]

- Leaders understand socialized power is more important than personalized power.

➤ Today you don't lead by command, you lead by consent. Consent derives from an ability to persuade.[144]

➤ The grace and power of civility are what distinguishes effective leaders.

➤ Leaders empower people to act on their own.

➤ Admirable leaders do right for a cause, and do right for the people pursuing it.

➤ Leaders must actively countervail the ivory tower syndrome that comes with elevation into senior ranks.

➤ Capable leaders develop a good sense of smell for misleading, incomplete, or biased info.

➤ Leaders can choose the hill they can die on, so choose battles wisely.

➤ Leaders always need a few trusted confidantes around them to offer unvarnished, candid feedback that others may be too afraid or polite to offer.

➤ Leaders must be willing to re-imagine and revise their criteria for success as they confront scale and scope challenges, new and more powerful players emerge onto the scene, and they face more complex dynamics up the career rungs.[145]

➤ Leaders look forward to interacting with people, not just when they have business to transact.

➤ Leaders are capable of exercising good and effective leadership regardless of rank, title, or position in the hierarchy.

➤ High-performing leaders practice the art of immaculate preparation.

➤ Leaders define reality and give hope.[146]

➤ The best leaders never stop learning.

➤ Leaders make people feel important.[147]

➤ Leaders demonstrate real concern for their subordinates.

➤ If you are a true leader, it is never about you.[148]

APPENDIX

"LAWS OF THE NAVY"

By Admiral R.A. Hopwood, Royal Navy

Now these are the laws of the Navy, Unwritten and varied they be; And he that is wise will observe them, Going down in his ship to the sea;

As naught may outrun the destroyer, Even so with the law and its grip, For the strength of the ship is the Service, And the strength of the Service the ship.

Take heed what ye say of your seniors, Be your words spoken softly or plain, Lest a bird of the air tell the matter, And so ye shall hear it again.

If ye labour from morn until even', And meet with reproof for your toil, It is well—that the guns be humbled - The compressor must check the recoil.

On the strength of one link of the cable, Dependeth the might of the chain. Who knows when thou mayest be tested? So live that thou bearest the strain!

When the ship that is tired returneth, With the signs of the sea showing plain, Men place her in dock for a season, And her speed she reneweth again.

So shall thou, lest perchance thou grow weary, In the uttermost parts of the sea, Pray for leave, for the good of the Service, As much and as oft as may be.

Count not upon certain promotion, But rather to gain it aspire; Though the sight-line end on the target, There cometh, perchance, a miss-fire.

If ye win through an Arctic ice floe, Unmentioned at home in the press, Heed it not—no man seeth the piston, But it driveth the ship none-the-less.

Can'st follow the track of the dolphin, Or tell where the sea swallows roam; Where leviathan taketh his pastime, What ocean he calleth his home?

Even so with the words of thy seniors, And the orders those words shall convey. Every law is as naught beside this one - "Thou shalt not criticize, but obey!"

Saith the wise, "How may I know their purpose?" Then acts without wherefore or why, Stays the fool but one moment to question, And the chance of his life passeth by.

Do they growl? It is well: be thou silent, So that work goeth forward amain; Lo, the gun throws her shot to a hair's breadth And shouteth, yet none shall complain.

Do they growl and the work be retarded? It is ill, speak, whatever their rank; The half-loaded gun also shouteth, But can she pierce armour with blank?

Doth the funnels make war with the paintwork? Do the decks to the cannon complain? Nay—they know that some soap and a scraper Unites them as brothers again.

So ye, being Heads of Departments, Do your growl with a smile on your lips, Lest ye strive and in anger be parted, And lessen the might of your ship.

Dost think, in a moment of anger, 'Tis well with thy seniors to fight? They prosper, who burn in the morning, The letters they wrote overnight.

For some there be, shelved and forgotten, With nothing to thank for their fate, Save that (on a half-sheet of foolscap,) Which a fool "Had the Honour to state—."

Dost deem that thy vessel needs gilding, And the dockyard forbear to supply? Place thy hand in thy pocket and gild her, There be those who have risen thereby.

If the fairway be crowded with shipping, Beating homeward the harbour to win, It is meet that, lest any should suffer, The steamers pass cautiously in.

So thou, when thou nearest promotion, And the peak that is gilded is nigh, Give heed to thy words and thine actions, Lest others be wearied thereby.

It is ill for the winners to worry. Take thy fate as it comes with a smile, And when thou art safe in the harbour, They will envy, but may not revile.

Uncharted the rocks that surround thee, Take heed that the channels thou learn, Lest thy name serve to buoy for another That shoal, the Courts-Martial Return.

Though Armour, the belt that protects her, The ship bears the scar on her side, It is well if the court acquit thee, It were best hadst thou never been tried.

Now these are the laws of the Navy, Unwritten and varied they be; And he that is wise will observe them, Going down in his ship to the sea.

As the wave rises clear to the hawse pipe, Washes aft, and is lost in the wake, So shall ye drop astern, all unheeded, Such time as the law ye forsake.

Now these are the laws of the Navy, And many and mighty are they, But the hull and the deck and the keel And the truck of the law is—OBEY!

First published in the British
"Army and Navy Gazette" in July 1896.

ENDNOTES

1   Aoibhinn McBridge. "Only 21% of U.S. Employees Trust the Leadership at Work." *The Hill*. Mar 12, 2023. Thehill.com cccessed January 18, 2024.

2   U.S. News and Harris Poll joint poll from November 2023. Usnews.com accessed on January 18, 2024.

3   U.S. News and Harris Poll joint poll from April 2023. Usnews.com accessed on January 18, 2024.

4   Gallup annual governance survey, September 2023. News.gallup.com accessed on January 18, 2024.

5   Mohammed Younis, "Confidence in the U.S. Military Lowest in Over Three Decades," *Gallup*, July 31, 2023. News.gallup.com accessed January 18 2024. Even though it is the lowest in years, the confidence level still registered at 60%, much higher than other federal organizations.

6   In *The Fourth Turning: What the Cycles of History Tell Us About America's Next Rendezvous with Destiny* (New York: Broadway Books, 1998), William Strauss and Neil Howe suggest the U.S. may only be awoken from its dangerous reverie by a wrenching upheaval, monumental crisis, or massive shock such as losing a war most Americans presume we are pre-ordained to win. Their historical review suggests that the only path to purge poor leaders from positions of power and revitalize society is to encounter a horrific reckoning. Based on cycles of history, the authors predict America will experience a major war with significant consequences sometime in the mid-2020s.

7   H. Jackson Brown. *P.S. I Love You*, 1990. Sarah was the author's mother. The quote is frequently misattributed to Mark Twain.

8   Avoidance of accountability is listed as one of Patrick Lencioni's *The Five Dysfunctions of a Team*. San Franciso: Jossey-Bass, 2002.

9   Inspired by Senator Alan Simpson's saying at George HW Bush's funeral that "hatred corrodes the container it is carried in."

10   Perry, Mark. *Eclipse: The Last Days of the CIA.* DIANE Publishing Company, 1992, p. 211.

11   As former CIA Director George Tenet later said about Charlie, "if we only had 100 more like you Charlie, we'd conquer all of our intelligence challenges." INSA tribute to Charlie Allen, 21 June 2023.

12   DHS amalgamated 22 different federal organizations when it was legislated into existence in 2003. Early on, vertical connections between local and national levels were fragmented and thin, at best slow. Relationships between government and private sector entities were spotty. At the executive level, DHS components were horizontally challenged, fiercely independent with legacy missions, cultures, processes, and incentive systems. Recall that one of the major findings of the 9/11 Commission was the failure to connect the dots on Al Qaeda's attack planning.

13   The nine entities included DHS headquarters Intelligence and Analysis, Coast Guard Intelligence, Customs and Border Protection Intelligence, Secret Service Intelligence, Transportation Security Administration Office of Intelligence, Federal Air Marshal Service Intelligence, Immigration and Customs Enforcement Intelligence, Federal Protective Service Intelligence, and Citizenship and Immigration Service Intelligence.

14   Coach Tony Dungy reminds in *Uncommon: Finding Your Path to Significance* (Carol Stream: Tyndall House Publishers, Inc, 2009, p. 14) that "integrity does not come in degrees—low, medium, or high. You either have integrity or you do not."

15   Ariella Ginzler, "Raven's Way." Outside, Trailrunner article from April 26, 2017.

16   Peter Vanham, "Five leadership lessons you can learn from a guy who runs 8 miles a day for 40 years." May 18, 2017. Accessed August 31, 2023 at https://www.cnbc.com/2017/05/18/5-leadership-lessons-you-can-learn-from-a-guy-whos-run-8-miles-every-day-for-40-years.html

17   According to Ginzler, Raven said "I love bringing people together and inspiring them to become stronger and healthier. It has become my mission and motivation." He also advised "keep it simple" and "everybody has a place where they shine."

18 Laura Lee Huttenbach's Book Club Review with *The Half Marathon* on March 15, 2020.

19 A Japanese business concept called Kaizen, which advocates small improvements daily. This concept was influenced by Dr. William Edwards Deming, who helped Japan rebuild and improve their manufacturing processes after World War II.

20 The best students tended to be Mormons who had joined the Army for the language opportunity, and who knew they would ultimately use Mandarin Chinese after their service commitments in pursuit of spreading the Gospel.

21 Some analysts speculated the Pakistan Intelligence Services may have masterminded the Parliament attacks to compel India's military to redeploy mountaineering and infantry battalions away from the Pakistan-Afghanistan border, allowing Osama Bin Laden to escape Tora Bora.

22 Admiral Faller would go on to become a four-star admiral and Combatant Commander of U.S. Southern Command. I proudly served as his Director of Intelligence (J2) for almost a year in the 2018–2019 timeframe.

23 Wikipedia. "The Ideological Leanings of Supreme Court Justices," 1950–2020 graphics. https://en.wikipedia.org/wiki/Ideological_leanings_of_United_States_Supreme_Court_justices. The article notes that the "nature of the cases the Supreme Court chooses to hear may lead the justices to appear more liberal or conservative than they would if they were hearing a different set of cases; the Court accepts only 100–200 of the more than 7,000 cases that it is asked to review each year."

24 See Donald T. Phillips *Lincoln on Leadership: Executive Strategies for Tough Times*, New York: Warner Books, 1992, pp. 76–83. Tom Peters's *Thriving On Chaos* (Harper Perennial, 2007) also outlines ways for leaders to best deal with the natural paradoxes of leadership.

25 I also turned down Fourth Fleet in Mayport, Florida responsible for the southern hemisphere of the Americas and Tenth Fleet in Ft. Meade, Maryland, which handled global cyber issues.

26 As G.K. Chesterton warned: "It will be an ironic tragedy if, when we have toiled to find rest, we find we are incurably restless. It will be sad if, when we have worked for our holiday, we find we have unlearnt everything but work. The typical modern man is the insane millionaire, who has

drudged to get his money, and then finds he cannot enjoy even money, but only drudgery." *The Apostle and the Wild Ducks*. Elek: London, 1975.

27   For more on this theme, see O'Neil, John R. *The Paradox of Success: When Winning at Work Means Losing at Life*. Tarcher Master Mind Editions. New York: G.P. Putnam's Sons, 1993.

28   For a more detailed description of JOTS, see https://ieeexplore.ieee.org/document/140395. Accessed September 1, 2023.

29   Akrivou, Kleio, Bourantas, Dimitrios, Mo, Shenjiang, Papalois, Evi, "The Sound of Silence-a Space for Morality: The Role of Solitude for Ethical Decision Making," Journal of Business Ethics, 2011, 102: pp. 119–133.

30   The phrase is commonly used in the Defense Department and Intelligence Community to mean staying within classified spaces and inside the realm of secrets. To see all the potential origins of the saying "behind the green door," see the Defense News article: https://breakingdefense.com/2019/09/the-green-door-mystery-solved-secrecy-slang/.

31   Intelligence professionals' fear of revealing classified information would be easily overcome if more intelligence personnel regularly consumed more open source materials and understand the vast amount of top cover that exists to talk about many issues. Intelligence officers do not need to reveal classified details, sources and methods, levels of certainty, nor specific knowns and unknowns in order to perform effective engagements in unclassified open fora.

32   I felt a special retrospective connection with my grandfather after a 48-hour stint riding a U.S. submarine from Gibraltar to La Maddalena Navy Base in northern Sardinia in 1994, plying the same waters he deployed in 50 years earlier. At the time, I was an intelligence briefer for coalition submarine missions in the Adriatic during the Balkan War.

33   See HMS *Sybil*'s logs at https://uboat.net/allies/warships/ship/3436.html. A Wikipedia history on HMS *Sybil* can be found at https://en.wikipedia.org/wiki/HMS_Sibyl_(P217). Accessed July 15, 2023.

34   John Prados, "The John Walker Spy Ring and the U.S. Navy's Biggest Betrayal." U.S. Naval Institute, September 2, 2014. Accessed July 24 2023 at https://news.usni.org/2014/09/02/john-walker-spy-ring-u-s-navys-biggest-betrayal

35   Joint interview with Rich Haver and Bill Studeman. September 1, 2023.

36   See FBI History at https://www.fbi.gov/history/famous-cases/year-of-the-spy-1985.

37   Rich Haver's bio was listed at a John Hopkins Applied Physics Lab conference on technology: see https://www.jhuapl.edu/colloquium/Archive/Detail?colloqid=170

38   Bobby Inman and Bill Studeman eventually became four-star admirals. They were the first and only two Naval Intelligence officers to ever achieve that rank.

39   Berkeley Law study prepared by Robert J. MacCoun and William M. Hix, Chapter 5 "Unit Cohesion and Military Performance." Accessed 18 August 2023 at https://www.law.berkeley.edu/files/csls/Unit_Cohesion_and_Military_Performance_Ch5_MacCoun_Hix.pdf

40   Richard A. Guzzo, Paul R. Yost, Richard J. Campbell, Gregory P. Shea, "Potency in Groups: Articulating a Construct." *British Journal of Social Psychology*. March 1993, Vol 32, Issue 1, pp. 87–106.

41   My Naval Postgraduate School thesis was called "Dragon in the Shadows: Calculating the Triggers for China's Advances in the South China Sea." An abridged version of it was published in the *Naval War College Review* in 1998.

42   For more on the NATO shoot downs, see details of the Banja Luka incident at https://en.wikipedia.org/wiki/Banja_Luka_incident Accessed on August 19, 2023.

43   Jack Woodford in *Strangers in Love* wrote, "few human beings are proof against the implied flattery of rapt attention." Cited in Dale Carnegie. *How to Win Friends and Influence People*, New York: Simon & Schuster, 1936.

44   Cohen, p. 53. A General warns against belittling a person to the point that they lose her or her self-respect, which in addition to doing undue personal harm, undermines a leader's ability to lead and influence that person from that point onward.

45   *In How Good People Make Tough Choices: Resolving the Dilemmas of Ethical Living* (New York: Harper Collins, 1995, pp. 182–183), author Dr. Rushworth M. Kidder offers right-wrong tests through which to judge

proper action. They include a legal test, regulations test, front-page test, Mom test, and a stench test. The latter relies on moral intuition, a gut-level determination, an inner sense that something is not right even though you can't quite put your finger on the problem.

46   Ludwig, D.C., Longenecker, C.O. "The Bathsheba Syndrome: The ethical failure of successful leaders." *J Bus Ethics* 12, 265–273 (1993). https://doi.org/10.1007/BF01666530.

47   Chief of Naval Operations memo to all prospective Commanding Officers titled "The Charge of Command" dated November 8, 2011. Accessed September 2023 at https://dnnlgwick.blob.core.windows.net/portals/16/the%20charge%20of%20command_11_8_2011_9_28_40.pdf?sr=b&si=DNNFileManagerPolicy&sig=nU2JyufQOyY0sce7F%2BQoBl6DBDXSZOETOatH%2FhKJsxU%3D

48   Captain Carey Cash, "Murphy's Law: Advice for Naval Leaders," *Proceedings*, February 2021, Vol 147/2/1.

49   Christine Porath and Christine Pearson, "The Price of Incivility," *Harvard Business Review*, January-February 2013 issue.

50   A Third Class Petty Officer is an E-4, or Enlisted rank on the fourth rung of nine possible rungs leading up to a Master Chief Petty Officer. A First Class Petty Officer is an E-6.

51   Wikipedia perfectly describes a military Mustang: "It refers to the mustang horse, a feral animal and therefore not a thoroughbred. A Mustang, after being captured, can be tamed and saddle broken, but it always has a bit of a wild streak, and can periodically revert to its old ways unexpectedly, and therefore the owner needs to keep an eye on it at all times. However, since a Mustang was formerly a feral and free animal, it may be smarter, more capable, and have a better survival instinct than thoroughbreds." https://en.wikipedia.org/wiki/Mustang_(military_officer). Accessed on 14 August, 2023.

52   See Brene Brown, *The Power of Vulnerability: Teachings on Authenticity, Connection, and Courage.* Audio book, released 24 May 2013. Her 2010 breakout book Gifts of Imperfection also addresses letting go of ones fears in order to connect.

53   If they had done their research, they would have found she was valedictorian of her high school class and a Phi Beta Kappa honor society

member from the College of William & Mary, where we met and fell in love when we were 19.

54   Useem, Michael, *Leading Up: How to Lead Your Boss So You Both Win*, New York: Three Rivers Press, 2001, p. 31.

55   Multiple voices encourage creating value for one's organization beyond your immediate job responsibilities, including Russ Benes who said: "Don't think that you always need to ask permission to add value in your job." Austin, p.12.

56   Cohen, on p. 127 reinforces the notion that a "bias for action is what your superior wants. Show initiative ... or your boss will soon search for others who are more willing to take charge."

57   This phenomenon is covered well in Nicholas Carr's *The Shallows: What the Internet is Doing to Our Brains*, New York: W.W. Norton and Company, 2011.

58   Harvey B. Mackay. *Swim with the Sharks Without Being Eaten Alive*. New York: William Morrow & Company, 1988. See Lesson 44 entitled "Your Best People May Spent Their Most Productive Time Starting at the Walls."

59   Cohen, pp. 187–188 provide a list of leading questions that may elicit useful feedback from subordinates.

60   Quote from Admiral Scott Stearney, who oversaw the CRIC on behalf of the CNO.

61   A famous slogan from classical Chinese history. Mao infamously used this quote in 1956 to lift restrictions on freedom of thought and speech, starting a short-lived campaign of openness before he viciously backtracked.

62   ISIL was originally called ISIS, which is still used by many international media outlets. Since 2014, the group has called itself the Islamic State (IS). For more details on the groups titles over time, see https://www.britannica.com/story/is-it-isis-or-isil.

63   Brene Brown in *Dare to Lead* points out that leaders "have to be vigilant about creating a culture in which people feel safe, seen, heard, and respected." p. 12.

64   Bill Bernach was an American advertising creative director.

65   In *Made to Stick* (New York: Random House, 2007), Chip Heath and Dan Heath highlight six principles of sticky ideas: simplicity, concreteness, emotion, unexpectedness, credibility, and stories.

66   Kerr, James. *Legacy: What the All Blacks Can Teach Us About the Business of Life*. Great Britain: Constable, 2013, pp. 157–165. This chapter explains how leaders and teams "ritualize to actualize;" in other words, use rituals to reinforce a group narrative and unite around a unique sense of identity.

67   Adam Bernstein, "Sumner Shapiro, Long-Serving Director of Naval Intelligence." *Washington Post* obituary, November 16, 2006.

68   Bill Studeman was one of the key officers working to "influence the Soviet strategic mindset" during peacetime. David A. Rosenberg, "The History of World War III, 1945–1990: A Conceptual Framework," in *On Cultural Ground: Essays in International History*, Robert David Johnson, ed., Imprint Studies in International Relations, 1 (Chicago: Imprint, 1994), p. 214.

69   Rear Admiral Bobby Inman was the brainchild of the Advanced Technology Panel (ATP), recommending this concept to the Chief of Naval Operations to bring sensitive intelligence to senior warfare officers shepherding major programs, like the Trident Sea-based Ballistic Missile, into the Navy.

70   John B. Hattendorf. "The Evolution of the U.S. Navy's Maritime Strategy, 1977–1986." Newport, Rhode Island: Center for Naval Warfare Studies, Naval War College, 1989.

71   According to Rich Haver, Admiral Harry Train commented in a Naval Intelligence briefing that revealed the actual Soviet mindset, "I should have known. The Russians see Naval strategy through the lens of a Field Marshal."

72   Comment by Rear Admiral Tom Brooks, a subsequent Director of Naval Intelligence, reflecting back on his Pentagon days working in the inner circle with Haver.

73   Central to the Navy's ability to get this intelligence was the ability to work intimately with the National Security Agency. Vice Admiral Bobby

Inman, Director of NSA at the time, proved pivotal in ensuring the Navy had access to NSA's signals intelligence teams and their collection results.

74   Admiral James D. Watkins, "The Maritime Strategy," U.S. Naval Institute *Proceedings*, January 1986, Vol.112/1/995 Supplement.

75   Vice Admiral (retired) Jake Jacoby describes the Navy being ordered to hold Soviet ballistic missile submarines at risk by having a U.S. submarine trail every SSBN while they were at sea. "Lessons Learned from the Cold War—Applications for Great Power Competition." Naval Intelligence Professionals *Readbook*, Volume IV, No.1, Spring/Summer 2023, p. 36.

76   The best accounting of this entire period in U.S. history can be found in Christopher Ford and David Rosenberg's *The Admiral's Advantage: U.S. Navy Operational Intelligence in World War II and the Cold War*. Annapolis: Naval Institute Press, 2005. See also Peter M. Swartz. "Understanding an Adversary's Strategic and Operational Calculus: a Late Cold War Case Study with 21st Century Applications." A Center for Naval Analysis monograph issued in August 2013. CNA analysts such as Robert Herrick and James McConnell had analyzed unclassified Soviet source materials in the 1970s and were the first to arrive at an understanding that Soviet doctrine was actually more defensive. But it took acquiring classified insights to corroborate those findings before the Navy and the Office of Naval Intelligence would alter their own institutional biases.

77   Phone interview with Rich Haver, 15 August 2023.

78   One of the best talent-finding methodologies is offered by Tom Rath in *Strengths Finder 2.0*, New York: Gallup Press, 2007.

79   Sanyin Siang, a leadership coach at Duke University, calls a person's natural talents "superpowers."

80   See China and Russia Cyber Threat Overviews and Advisories. Cybersecurity and Infrastructure Security Agency. https://www.cisa.gov/topics/cyber-threats-and-advisories/advanced-persistent-threats/china

81   Chinese penetration into the U.S. companies, universities, research labs, and government institutions remains a largely taboo subject in the U.S. China has been energetic in exploiting our open society to their benefit. Chinese intelligence agents will approach Americans of Chinese descent and appeal to their heritage to solicit cooperation. Chinese spies also use

a well-worn technique of threatening any family members still in China to secure support for their collection objectives.

82   Commission on the Theft of American Intellectual Property reports. Studies chaired by Dennis Blair and co-chaired by Jon Huntsman, Jr. The National Bureau of Asian Research, May 2013 and February 2017.

83   General Alexander remarks at the American Enterprise Institute, July 2012.

84   George Mason University National Security Archive. "USCYBERCOM After Action Assessment of Operation Glowing Symphony." Released January 21, 2020. Accessed 17 August 2023 at https://nsarchive.gwu. edu/briefing-book/cyber-vault/2020–01–21/uscybercom-after-action-assessments-operation-glowing-symphony

85   Dina Temple-Raston. "How the U.S. Hacked ISIS." NPR. September 26, 2019. Accessed 18 August at https://www.npr.org/2019/09/26/763545811/how-the-u-s-hacked-isis

86   Captain Phillips was aware of official warnings to stay 600nm from the Somali coast based on the well-known dangers of piracy in the area. This incident could have been avoided if those notices had been heeded.

87   In the months prior to USS *Bainbridge*'s deployment and knowing the destroyer would assume a number of transnational missions off the Horn of Africa, I worked with the ship's skipper, Captain Castellano, to improve the destroyer crew's readiness. We coordinated with the SEAL community to emplace a Special Warfare network on the ship. As N2, my team also arranged analytic experts from the National Counterterrorism Center and Defense Counterterrorism Center to ride the ship for many weeks to provide instant, on-hand deep knowledge of the region.

88   Cohen, William A, Ph.D., Major General USAF (ret), *The New Art of the Leader*, Paramus: Prentice Hall Press, 2000, p. 233. "If you make indecisiveness a habit, your people will not want to follow you. Failing to make a decision is also a decision. It is a decision to leave everything to chance or to the initiative of others." See also Noel M. Tichy and Stratford Sherman's book *Control Your Destiny or Someone Else Will* (New York: Collins, 2005).

89   "China's loss of soldiers during Galwan clash nine-times more than its official count," The Economic Times, February 3, 2022. Accessed

September 13, 2023 at https://economictimes.indiatimes.com/news/defence/china-suffered-higher-losses-than-reported-australian-news-paper-on-galwan-valley-clash/articleshow/89308159.cms?from=mdr

90   Chellaney, Brahma (19 December 2022). "Modi's silence on China's land grabs will not be India's last word—*Nikkei Asia*. Peri, Vijaita Singh & Dinakar (24 January 2023). "India has lost access to 26 out of 65 Patrolling Points in Eastern Ladakh." *The Hindu*.

91   Paul D. Shinkman, "U.S. Intel Helped Rout China in 2022 Border Clash," U.S. News & World Report, March 20, 2023. Arpan Rai "US intelligence helped prevent China incursion into India," *Independent*, March 21, 2023. Jim Garamone, "U.S., India Ties Continue to Strengthen, Austin Says," U.S. Department of Defense official website, September 26, 2022. https://www.defense.gov/News/News-Stories/Article/Article/3170929/us-india-ties-continue-to-strengthen-austin-says/

92   Captain Himadri Das, "Maritime Domain Awareness in India: Shifting Paradigms," National Maritime Foundation, September 30, 2021. Vicky Nanjappa, "BECA to MISTA: How India, US are enhancing intel sharing on the high seas," OneIndia, December 7, 2020. Accessed September 12, 2023 at https://www.oneindia.com/beca-to-mista-how-india-us-are-enhancing-maritime-intel-sharing-on-the-high-seas-cs-3185991.html

93   The Hawaiians use the word "laulima" to describe "cooperation, joint action; a group of people working together; community; to work together." See the University of Hawaii site: https://www.hawaii.edu/news/2023/09/19/hawaiian-word-of-the-week-laulima/. One of my former executive assistants, Army Major Truong Tran, initiated a Laulima Series on Leadership with the 500th Military Intelligence Brigade on Oahu.

94   Juhohn Lee. "America has spent over a trillion dollars fighting the war on drugs. 50 years later, drug use in the U.S. is climbing again." CNBC policy article, June 17, 2021.

95   Admiral Kurt Tidd testimony to Congress 2017.

96   World Report. Venezuela events 2017, 2018, 2019. http://hrw.org. Accessed August 29, 2023.

97   Joe Carrasco. "Venezuelan Democracy was Strangled by Cuba." *Foreign Policy*, May 14, 2019.

98   Alessandra Soler. "Is China exporting its surveillance state to Venezuela?" *Global Voices*, September 28, 2021.

99   As of 2023, seven million people from Venezuela's population of 32 million have fled the country, pressurizing neighboring countries in the Caribbean and South America. Colombia alone has taken in almost two million.

100   Reinhold Neibuhr's 1932 serenity prayer: "God grant me the serenity to accept the things I cannot change, courage to change the things I can, and wisdom to know the difference."

101   Captain Edwin Layton was Admiral Chester Nimitz's senior intelligence officer who predicted the Japanese attack on Midway and provided specific warning details that enabled the U.S. Navy to surprise the Imperial Navy and turn the tide of the war in the Pacific. Captain Layton had lived in Japan, spoke Japanese, and knew many Imperial Navy officers. Layton predicted the arrival of the Japanese around Midway to the exact day, hour, and location. Layton later became an admiral.

102   "The cave you fear holds the treasure you seek," a saying commonly ascribed to Joseph Campbell.

103   Too often, other intelligence professionals at forward locations at sea, in maritime operations centers at Numbered Fleets, or in Joint Intelligence Operations Centers were forced to excavate ONI's multi-page products and repackage them to meet their actual needs, placing additional burdens on already task-saturated intelligence teams.

104   Rear Admiral Mike Studeman. "A Navigation Fix from COMONI," Naval Intelligence Professionals *Readbook*, Volume III, No.2, Fall/Winter 2022, pp. 3–4.

105   Sometimes DIME is expanded to DIMEFIL, adding Financial, Intelligence, and Law Enforcement instruments.

106   Andrea Worden, "China Pushes 'Human Rights with Chinese Characteristics' at the UN," China Change, October 9, 2017. https://chinachange.org/2017/10/09/china-pushes-human-rights-with-chinese-characteristics-at-the un/#:~:text=Despite%20the%20fact%20that%20the,development%20and%20economic%20rights%20over

107   Jude Blanchette and Seth G. Jones, "Beijing's New Narrative of U.S. Decline," Center for Strategic and International Studies, July 1, 2021.

108   Kenton Thibaut, "Chinese Discourse Power: Ambitions and Reality in the Digital Domain," Atlantic Council, August 24, 2022.

109   Alexander Bowe, "China Overseas United Front Work: Background and Implications for the United States," U.S.-China Economic and Security Review Commission, August 24, 2018. Report accessed September 12, 2023 at https://www.uscc.gov/research/chinas-overseas-united-front-work-background-and-implications-united-states

110   Steven W. Mosher covers all these matters in detail in *Bully of Asia: Why China's Dream is the New Threat to World Order*, Washington D.C.: Regnery Publishing, 2017.

111   Kai Strittmatter describes life in China's surveillance state in *We Have Been Harmonized*, New York: HarperCollins Publisher, 2018.

112   Betsy Woodruff Swan and Bryan Bender. "Spy Chiefs Look to Declassify Intelligence After Rare Pleas from 4-star Commanders." Politico, April 26, 2021. See also intelligence leaders' testimony submitted to the House Armed Services Committee, Subcommittee on Intelligence and Special Operations, on "Disinformation in the Gray Zone." March 16, 2021.

113   For more information on systematic organizational renovations, see Kevin Oakes *Culture Renovation: 18 Leadership Actions to Build an Unshakeable Company*, New York: McGraw Hill, 2021.

114   Phrases coined by Joshua Cooper Ramo in *The Age of the Unthinkable: Why the New World Disorder Constantly Surprises Us*, New York: Back Bay Books, 2009.

115   Mao Zedong told President Nixon in 1972, "We can wait, maybe even a hundred years" to reunify Taiwan. "Someday we will ask for it, but we do not need to discuss it at this moment."

116   This attitude is sometimes described as Stockdale's Paradox after Vice Admiral James Stockdale, a naval aviator who survived as a prisoner of war in Vietnam, inspiring others to resist and persist, which earned him a Congressional Medal of Honor. Stockdale said, "You must never confuse faith that you will prevail in the end—which you can never

afford to lose—with the discipline to confront the most brutal facts of your current reality, whatever they might be."

117   See Taleb, Nassim Nicholas, *The Black Swan: The Impact of the Highly Improbable*, New York: Random House, 2007, p. 11, p. 204.

118   For more on taking charge of your destiny in the face of discontinuous change, see Handy, Charles, *The Age of Unreason*, Boston: Harvard Business School Press, 1990. Jack Welch also said "A leader's job is to look into the future and see the organization, not as it is, but as it should be."

119   Gary Hamel and C. K. Prahalad in *Competing for the Future* (Brighton, MA: Harvard Business Review, 1996) agree that "seeing the future first may be more about having a wide-angle lens than a crystal ball."

120   In *Tyranny of the Minority*, Steven Levitsky and Daniel Ziblatt, who are Harvard professors of government, convincingly show America is structurally flawed in ways that increasingly lock-in minority rule by a single and radicalized partisan party. They highlight that democracies cannot survive with excessively counter-majoritarian institutions that define American government today. "It's not unfettered majorities that threaten us today. It's *fettered majorities* that are the problem." New York: Crown, 2023, pp 164.

121   Stewart Emery and Ivan Misner. *Who's in Your Room? The Question That Will Change Your Life*. Oakland, CA: Berrett-Koehler Publishers, Inc, 2023, p. 17.

122   Bennis, Warren, *On Becoming a Leader*, Cambridge: Perseus Publishing, 1994. Mr Bennis and the late Peter Drucker have been most commonly quoted using this phrase.

123   Covey, p. 148.

124   Covey, p. 237.

125   Austin, p.28.

126   Covey, p. 83.

127   Sinek, Simon. *The Infinite Game*. London: Portfolio/Penguin, 2019.

128 Collins, Jim, *Good to Great: Why Some Companies Make the Leap ... And Others Don't*, New York: Harper Collins Publishing, 2001.

129 Heraclitus is said to have originally described the concept that "Everything flows, nothing stands still," which has also been translated as "All is flux, nothing is stationary."

130 Collins, Jim, "Aligning Actions and Values," The Forum, June 2000. jim. collins.com/article topics/ articles/aligning_action.html.

131 Parker, Sam, *212 The Extra Degree*, Bedford: The Walk the Talk Company, 2005.

132 Marlow Hicks in Austin, p.115.

133 Covey, p. 283.

134 Denney, James., Denney, Jim., Williams, Pat. *Coach Wooden: The 7 Principles That Shaped His Life and Will Change Yours*. United States: Baker Publishing Group, 2011. p.180.

135 Powell, Colin. *My American Journey* (New York: Random House, 1995), p. 613.

136 Epitaph of a UK Major and member of the Royal family killed in France in 1944.

137 I first heard this phrase from Captain (future Rear Admiral) Richard Porterfield during his welcome aboard indoctrination talk at the Joint Intelligence Center, Pacific in 1999.

138 Collins, Chapter 8.

139 Martin Luther King Jr speech in 1968.

140 Kerr, p. 35.

141 Sinek, p. xiii.

142 Kerr, p. 3.

143 Brene, p. 77.

144 Albert Einstein agreed stating "The led must not be compelled, they must be able to choose their own leader."

145   Gary Benson of Ethox Corporation admitted he had to change his "fierce independence for interdependence" to effectively get things done with other people the more senior he became. Austin, p.130.

146   Napoleon Bonaparte once said, "A leader is a dealer in hope."

147   Cosmetics Founder Mary Kay Ash often told audiences that everyone has an invisible sign hanging from their necks saying "MAKE ME FEEL IMPORTANT."

148   Cohen, "If you are a real leader, your own personal interests come dead last," p. 173.

ACKNOWLEDGMENTS

To all the Navy and joint service officers, enlisted, and civilian leaders I had the honor of serving with over the course of a long career who set the example for how to lead well and effectively through challenging times. To Admiral (retired) Sandy Winnefeld for reading my earliest manuscript draft and advising me to find the courage to tell personal stories and breathe life into leadership lessons found in my "minutes." He inspired authorship with his own memoir *Sailing Upwind*. To my squadron mate Greg Glaros, a former Navy Captain and industry CEO, for his constant encouragement to bring the book's message to the public and his astute editing calls, especially recommendations on reworking the chapter structure. To Ensign Matthew King for his editing prowess as a superb writer in his own right and generous facilitation in placing my manuscript in front of Dr. Kissinger, one of the last ones he read before passing. To Admiral (retired) Craig Faller for cautioning me to save my manifesto for later, offering valuable recommendations, and sharing his surface warfare officer enthusiasm for weaving more nautical themes in the book. To Frank Gren for his advice to fiercely streamline. To Carrie and Maddie Murphy for sharing their cherished collection of personal testimonials about Steve's life and friendships. To Tim Demy for his early and continuing passion to collaborate on producing a book worth reading. To Amy Cole for her creative genius in graphic design. To Amy Dassler for sharing her artistic eye as we aesthetically refined the book cover. To Ian Ellis for his social media savvy and technical skills in developing ways to connect this book with interested readers. To Peter Singer for insightful coaching tips on publishing and marketing. And to my patient and loving wife, Lynne, who shaped the crafting of this work. Her instincts about what is always right and good have guided my every journey in life."

ABOUT THE AUTHOR

Mike Studeman is a retired Rear Admiral with three and a half decades of leadership experience and extensive acumen in intelligence, foreign policy, and defense matters. He has led and commanded thousands of intelligence professionals in turbulent times from high-stakes competitions to crises to war.

As a mid-grade officer, Mike was appointed by the President as a White House Fellow, the nation's premier leadership program for leadership and public service. He served as special assistant and brain trust leader for the Navy's top four-star flag officer leaders before assuming commands of major Navy and Joint service intelligence organizations himself. His assignments as an admiral include Director of Intelligence for U.S. Southern Command, Director of Intelligence for U.S. Indo-Pacific Command, National Intelligence Manager for global maritime matters for the Director of National Intelligence, and Commander of the Office of Naval Intelligence.

Mike comes from a family of military leaders from two countries. His father, Bill, was a four-star Admiral, former Director of the National Security Agency (NSA) and Deputy Director of Central Intelligence in the 1990s. His paternal grandfather was a fighter pilot in the Army Air Corps in the 1930s and later executive vice president of Pan Am. His maternal grandfather was a submariner in the Royal Navy during World War II.

Mike's alma mater is the College of William and Mary. He is an Honors Graduate in Mandarin Chinese from the Defense Language Institute, a Distinguished Graduate in National Security from the National War College, and a Distinguished Graduate in National Security Affairs from the Naval Postgraduate School. He is married to his college sweetheart and is the proud father of two boys.